DELICIOUS *For Fun!* REFRESHING

LARGE PRINT
CROSSWORDS

38

LARGE PRINT CROSSWORD PUZZLES

EDITED BY TIMOTHY E. PARKER

creative EDGE

Copyright © 2010 Universal Uclick

Distributed by Creative Edge, LLC. Franklin, TN 37068-2068 · 1-800-815-8696
Printed in the U.S.A.

18982/0510 — FRESH LARGE PRINT CROSSWORDS, VOLUME 1

1 Over Yonder

by Casey Rumblach
Edited by Timothy E. Parker

Copyright © 2010 Universal Uclick

ACROSS

1 Distinctive doctrines
5 Pinochle combos
10 Word with "side" or "satellite"
14 It comes on 10-Across
15 Numskull
16 Letter from Greece
17 Trujillo locale
18 Bowed instrument
19 Chaotic happenings
20 Some relatives
23 Omega's opposite
24 Trader's word
25 Tierra ___ Fuego
26 MGM lion
27 No spring chicken
30 What we have here
32 Settle (into)
34 Expungement
38 Exotic destinations
42 Bait fish

43 It might be skinned in the fall
45 Offered one's seat
48 Computer key
50 Sieging weapon
51 Fun-house cries
52 Target of fawning
56 Parts of molecules
58 Gizmos for couch potatoes
62 "Who Framed Roger Rabbit" character
63 Scent source
64 Like some singing
66 Gaelic tongue
67 Even the score again
68 Moose, for one
69 Hair salon stock
70 Took second, in a way
71 Withered

DOWN
1 Gremlin
2 Cotyledon
3 Lily plant
4 Not-so-pretty snow
5 Thin-leaved mineral
6 Setting in Haydn's "The Creation"
7 Lively songs
8 Gabbana's partner
9 Seat without a back
10 "Buenos ___!"
11 Salt of element 53
12 Paving pieces

13 Pester
21 Certain religious ideal
22 Radical
23 Draft choice?
28 Lecherous
29 Wind resistance
31 Undeleted expletive
33 Word in a Descartes conclusion
35 Nautical affirmative
36 TV commercial
37 An arm bone
39 Taxpayer's nightmare
40 Register signer
41 Tailor
44 They're worth three points in Scrabble
45 Performed a data-base operation
46 Hypothesis
47 Be absorbed slowly
49 Cordial surroundings?
53 Darling people
54 Double quartet
55 Drawing interesting to many?
57 Grown-up polliwogs
59 Low-value wad
60 Accomplish flaw-lessly
61 It leaves in spring time
65 Vein glory

2 It'll Grow on You

by Leana Bloom
Edited by Timothy E. Parker

Copyright © 2010 Universal Uclick

ACROSS

1 Plant deeply (Var.)
6 Self-help level
10 Hare tail, e.g.
14 Mother-in-law of Ruth
15 Lot measurement
16 Backside
17 Online activities
18 Start of a quote for mature solvers
20 "___ gratia artis"
21 Guitar legend Atkins
23 Snoopy sorts (Var.)
24 Provokes
26 X, in old Rome
27 Cyclotron particle
28 Flier Corrigan's nickname
33 Transit map markings
36 Tender legbone
37 Verdi opera
38 Middle of the quote
41 Ending with "buck" or "stink"
42 Sea in Antarctica

43 Reagan Cabinet member Ed

44 Narcotic drug

46 Signature piece?

47 First lady

48 Patient's problem

52 Containing neither flesh nor its juices

56 Popular belief

57 Networked computers, for short

58 End of the quote

60 ___ fro

62 Caffeine source, often

63 Cabinetmaker's tool

64 Jay Silverheels role

65 Was acquainted with

66 Spinning toy

67 Bend into an arch

DOWN

1 Machu Picchu resident, once

2 Olympic skiing medalist Phil

3 Do some chest-thumping

4 911 responder, briefly

5 Reveal

6 Hotel conveniences

7 Horseback ride

8 Poetically always

9 Caller's instrument, perhaps

10 Dog show command

11 Medical breakthrough

12 Cold War participant

13 The item here

19 Moran of "Happy Days"

22 Mother ptarmigan, e.g.

25 Highest point

26 New parents' purchases

28 "___ Life Is It Anyway?"

29 Soft blue-gray mineral

30 Expansive

31 Sweetened fruit beverages

32 Easily maneuverable, as a vessel

33 Used the pool

34 Poi source

35 ___ about (approximately)

36 Fourteen pounds, in Britain

39 One place to park the car

40 Brunch fare

45 White-hat wearer, stereotypically

46 For each

48 Juliet's love

49 Try this if things don't work out

50 ___ Domingo

51 Provide income for

52 Kind of truck

53 Shakespearean "soon"

54 Not up to much

55 Emulate a beaver

56 Shiftless

59 Words before a kiss

61 ___-pah-pah (tuba tune)

by Lewis Graham
Edited by Timothy E. Parker

ACROSS

1 Mambo relative
6 Part of a profit calculation
10 Talk casually
14 Newton of gravity fame
15 Cambodia's continent
16 Add punch to punch?
17 Horse blanket
18 Large quantity
19 On the sheltered side
20 Oppose
23 Keep under control
25 Deli bread
26 Tossed cube
27 Get a lode of this
28 Cardiology concern
31 Cake portion
33 Drying chamber
35 Snooker stick
36 Commandment violation
37 Wall Street fixture
42 Pit stop commodity
43 Rue Morgue culprit
44 Needing liniment, e.g.

46 Earth bound?
49 King David output
51 It's next to nothing?
52 Lifting device
53 It's after sigma
55 Structure for climbing
57 With a large trunk?
61 Continental currency
62 Satisfactory
63 Allowances for waste
66 Web filter target
67 "Present" alternative
68 Internet message
69 Suckers
70 Instruments of war
71 Peppy gathering

DOWN

1 Wheel part
2 "Born in the ___"
3 Most macho
4 Conductor's stick
5 Source of gum arabic
6 Simplest form of payment
7 Norwegian seaport
8 Rugged mountain range
9 Yellow-brown
10 Lobster's pride
11 Compound with a halogen atom
12 Acid found in vinegar
13 Giggle
21 Disparages
22 Art photo shade
23 Eeyore's bookmate
24 Notable times
29 Wish things otherwise

30 28th state
32 Cozy country lodges
34 Roman robe
36 Conchs, e.g.
38 Hindu social group
39 Apr. workhorse
40 What a poker player may seek
41 Long-winged sea eagle
45 Poetically "always"
46 Sisters' superior
47 Severe emotional shock
48 Thrash
49 React to a lemon
50 Substance
54 Hawaiian "hello"
56 Inner layer of the skin (Var.)
58 Deteriorates
59 Damage
60 Peepers
64 '___ death do us…"
65 Like a fox

4 Place Your Bets

Edited by Timothy E. Parker

Copyright © 2010 Universal Uclick

ACROSS

1 "Wine" partner
5 Hard work
9 Toots one's own horn
14 Dumb ___ ox
15 Outstanding
16 Provide with another point?
17 Speaks the unvarnished truth
20 Schoolyard taunts
21 Blows one's top
22 "Roll Over Beethoven" group.
23 Singer Bonnie
24 Puts it on the line (with 47-Across)
28 Word with "curtain" or "fist"
32 "Now ___ seen everything!"
33 Conditional words
34 Like winter in Buffalo
36 Syringe contents, perhaps
38 Fore opposite

40 You could get hit there
41 Stomach divisions, in some animals
43 Unhurried gait
45 Ma Bell
46 Goblet feature
47 See 24-Across
50 One way to set a clock
52 TV dinner morsel, perhaps
53 Enjoying continuing success
56 Delinquent
60 Bets the farm
62 Swift
63 Zeno's home
64 Early Icelandic prose
65 Remarkable deeds
66 Drinks politely
67 Belmonts frontman

DOWN
1 "The Persistence of Memory" painter
2 "No man ___ island"
3 Negative votes
4 Comes as a result
5 Bicep decorations
6 What's needed to go from millionaire to billionaire
7 Room offerer
8 Deadly
9 Top point of a mountain
10 Kinsman
11 Ear-related
12 Drunkard
13 Gush out

18 Infamy
19 Catches a cabbie's eye
23 Sold chances
24 Central points
25 In plain view
26 Uncanny, and a bit spooky
27 Narrow inlet
29 Fit for a king
30 Address an audience
31 They're out on a limb
35 Highest mountain
37 Not easily affordable
39 Dick and Harry's partner
42 Engraved marker
44 Juicy fruits
48 Even splits
49 Took to the tub
51 Masters of ceremonies
53 "Carmina Burana" composer Carl
54 Cairo Opera House location
55 Between ports
56 Kind of school
57 "___ do that?" (Steve Urkel's question)
58 Edit menu option
59 "Magnet and Steel" singer Walter
61 Wallach or Whitney

5 To a T

by Lucky Barrett
Edited by Timothy E. Parker

ACROSS

1 Ballet move with bended knees
5 Expensive car trips?
9 Where it all begins
14 "Five Women" author Jaffe
15 Smell ___ (suspect something)
16 In the beaver state?
17 Redundant partner of "done with"
18 It's better than never?
19 Strong adhesive
20 Grammarian's concern, perhaps
23 Displayed sudden interest, in a way
24 Capital near Lillehammer
25 Special gift
28 Mythomaniac
30 Better
33 Grp. that whistled "Dixie"?
36 Shearing sound

38 It may have a cross to bear
39 Constitutional guarantee
43 Imp's opposite
44 Verbal attack
45 Suffix with "computer"
46 Old British gold coins worth 21 shillings
49 Indochinese republic
51 Moscow-to-Baghdad dir.
52 Legendary first name in sitcoms
54 Small cuts
58 If you make this, there can be no possible change
61 Express verbally
64 Optimistic, as an outlook
65 Emotional request
66 Dough
67 Canal of song
68 Right-angle bends
69 Art of verse
70 D'Urbervilles miss
71 "Portnoy's Complaint" author

DOWN
1 Actors handle them
2 "I ___ Parade"
3 Quiescent
4 A load of gossip
5 It's softer than gypsum
6 "Messiah," for one
7 Charlie of the Rolling Stones
8 Addison's writing partner
9 Visualizes
10 Runner's destination

11 "... and seven years ___"
12 T. follower
13 Determine judicially
21 New Testament letter
22 Palindromic prefix
25 ___ nous (confidentially)
26 Confidence games
27 In and of itself
29 Member of a colony
31 Concord
32 ___ mode
33 Steep rocks
34 Skull cavity
35 Playing marble
37 TV network letters
40 Cooped-up female?
41 ...
42 Battery size
47 Nabokov heroine
48 Whispered item
50 Smile derisively
53 Salt away
55 Jacqueline Du Pre's instrument
56 Kowtowed, e.g.
57 Hidden supply
58 Serpentine swimmers
59 Doctored photo?
60 Motion-carrying votes
61 You could be safe with him
62 Overly
63 Darned spot?

by Alice Walker
Edited by Timothy E. Parker

ACROSS

1 Croatian, e.g.
5 Ghostly in appearance
10 Perplexing path
14 Street corner call
15 Unwavering look
16 Vehicle for hitting high notes, perhaps
17 "Be it ___ so humble ..."
18 Goatlike antelope
19 Some reading areas
20 Underdog's motivation (Part 1)
23 Extremist's prefix
24 Collect
25 Mixtures of metals
28 Baskin-Robbins purchase
30 Some forest animals
31 Enthusiastic approval
33 It may be a victim of blight
36 Underdog's motivation (Part 2)

40 Mary's Knight
41 Car protector
42 Type of pricing
43 Propagated
44 Not quite a sentence
46 Africa's largest city
49 Sound of an undignified
   landing
51 Underdog's motivation
   (Part 3)
57 Kin of hot pants
58 Art photo shade
59 It may form underground
   connections
60 Loving god of myth
61 Deal prerequisites,
   sometimes
62 Mark's replacement
63 Network of veins, e.g.
64 "Cabaret" director
65 Slumgullion

DOWN
1 Move a foot
2 Magma on the surface
3 They may go to blazes
4 Whiz
5 Owned properties, e.g.
6 Brenda the reporter
7 Port city north of Tel Aviv
8 Conclusion starter
9 Approach
10 Tussaud's title
11 Sports locale
12 Magnesium relatives
13 Assuages
21 Tissue layer
22 Ray of the tropics

25 Entrance for
   extraction
26 Misplace
27 Front the money
28 Bisque morsel,
   perhaps
29 Boathouse item
31 "My word!"
32 Junkyard canine
33 Vesuvius relative
34 Floral circles
35 Parcel (with "out")
37 Predictable cards?
38 Pilsner alternative
39 Fosters
43 Wound
44 The magic word
45 Is laid up with
46 Promising new arrival
47 Belching flames
48 "Otherwise ..."
49 Clan divisions
50 Uses a crowbar on
52 Mil. branch
53 It's full of slots
54 Vulgarian
55 Came apart at the
   seams, e.g.
56 Stick overhead, e.g.

by Lester Mapple
Edited by Timothy E. Parker

ACROSS

1 Move on ahead
5 Box score data
10 "I'll ____ brief as possible"
14 Epithet of Athena
15 Contents of some booths
16 Angle between a branch and stem
17 Hard, sweet treat
19 Not lethargic
20 By the year
21 Kind of wool
23 1002, to Nero
24 Neuters, as a horse
26 "Leave It to Beaver" character
28 Likely ____ (with equal probability)
30 Oft-used article
32 Pig ____ poke
33 One was civil in America
35 Mermaid's home
36 "Don't delete this"

37 It's hard to say
41 Men-children
42 Type of league
43 Grazing land
44 Org. overseeing summer and winter competitions
45 It's for the money
46 Crustaceans with stalked eyes
50 "The Republic" writer
52 Less likely to be found
56 Tell's home canton
57 Theatrical hit
59 Bengal tiger, for one
61 "___ a Lady" (Tom Jones)
62 Thing that's hard to miss
64 Lively and jaunty
65 Fiddle of yore
66 Statistics calculation
67 "An apple ___ ..."
68 Get the ball rolling
69 Gaelic tongue

DOWN

1 Kind of top or part
2 "Jagged Little Pill" singer Morissette
3 Like many coat linings
4 "Jungle Book" star
5 Upright stone slab
6 "...and ___ a good-night"
7 Resin in adhesives and paints
8 Rat tail?
9 Some Eur. Union members, once
10 Headquartered
11 Speed the progress of

12 Large passenger plane
13 Underhanded
18 Disorderly
22 Kind of square
25 Dwell on anger
27 Break bread
29 Has possession of
31 Icy precipitation
34 "Wrack" partner
35 Place of much wallowing
36 Luminary
37 Digs for a pick and shovel?
38 Being shot
39 "For," "how" or "what" ending
40 Skeleton in the closet, e.g.
41 Enjoy a quaff
45 Agents like Bond
47 Anonymous one, sometimes
48 Livestock lineages
49 Slangy ending for "yes" or "no"
51 Savory
53 Biology 101 subject (Var.)
54 Indy 500 competitor
55 Make into law
58 The lady's
60 Summit
61 Where some losers hang out?
63 "Are we there ___?"

Copyright © 2010 Universal Uclick

ACROSS

1 Speak in Spanish
6 Sherry bar appetizer, perhaps
10 Corkboard item
14 Dim
15 Surfer's diary
16 Wind in the pit?
17 Box office draw who doesn't act
20 Aucklander, casually
21 Roman goddess of plenty
22 Puppies' cries
23 Bobbsey twin
25 Some ostentatious outerwear
27 Shirt stainer, often
34 Need medical attention
35 Golden Rule word
36 Nearly extinct
38 Ditsy

40 Turn state's evidence
41 Wild and menacing
42 Type of salad
43 Niblick and brassie relative
45 Kind of meeting
46 Place to get some air
49 Chaucer offering
50 Drop the ball, e.g.
51 "Frutti" intro
54 With mouth shut
56 Seagirt land
60 Lawn staple in the Southwest
64 Elemental particle
65 Wee bit
66 First-string group
67 Used cars?
68 Point-of-honor settler
69 Energetic

DOWN
1 Corn residue
2 Proposal opposer
3 Botched
4 It can have a high cost
5 Had egg in one's face?
6 Recipe amt., perhaps
7 Italian high spots
8 Island dish
9 Delicate subject, to some
10 Without doubt
11 First victim
12 CEO's domain
13 They keep your powder dry
18 Trio of trios
19 Vega's constellation

24 Call from the crow's nest
25 Long, narrow estuaries
26 Letters on some ships
27 Pretzel add-on
28 Devoutly religious
29 Single-handedly
30 Ancient land east of Macedonia
31 Kid
32 Groups of wrist bones
33 Keats' muse
37 Distinctive flair
39 Kind of worker
41 Phobia
43 1/1000 inch
44 Checkout units
47 Conceited
48 Mournful in Marseilles
51 Ivan or Peter, e.g.
52 "I've had it ___ here!"
53 Trampled
54 Parcel (with "out")
55 Kazakhstan river
57 How-to part
58 Kind of year
59 Small-screen trophy
61 "The Karate ___" (1984)
62 Bud's funny buddy
63 Big, fat mouth

9 Great Ex-speck-tations

by Mark Milhet
Edited by Timothy E. Parker

ACROSS

1 Ritzy health resorts
5 One may have only one big part
10 Suck wind
14 It may have fallen on a foot
15 "The Rural Muse" poet
16 One of 50 in a united group
17 Nick's spouse, in film
18 Jack-in-the-pulpit cousin
19 Indian helmet
20 What 5-Across may sometimes wear
23 Playable serves
24 Ship deck
25 Turkish Angora, for one
28 Inscribe
31 State-of-the-art
35 Oil well fire fighter of note
37 First-rate
39 A big fan of

40 Pilot's boundary
43 Joule fractions
44 Lowly laborer
45 "I don't know" gesture
46 Speak sharply to
48 Cones partners
50 Tommy has a couple
51 Chop copy
53 Japanese delicacy
55 Potential start-up
62 Notice of demise, briefly
63 Column style
64 To ___ (precisely)
66 "Father" prefix
67 Supercilious
68 Did in the dragon
69 Chicken dinner?
70 Olympic measure
71 Legendary entertainer

DOWN
1 ___ Francisco 49ers
2 Theatrical object
3 Part of a large plot?
4 The voice of Lamb Chop
5 Greet obtrusively
6 Not bare
7 Baby-powder ingredient
8 Ship deck
9 Syllogist
10 Tolerate
11 Mite
12 Neck feature
13 That alternative
21 Like neon
22 Ballerina's perch
25 Some lighthouse sites
26 Bedeck

27 North American and Eurasian forest
29 Tearoom relative
30 Kind of "system" or "society"
32 Habituate (Var.)
33 Play, as a mandolin
34 Hinged kitchen utensils
36 Scrutinized
38 Taboo
41 The search for the silver lining
42 German steel city
47 Brouhaha
49 Rear window feature in some cars
52 Delmonico alternative
54 Pet checker
55 Tip, as a topper
56 Clarinet cousin
57 Kind of iron
58 "One Adam Twelve," e.g.
59 Rectangle part
60 French town of WWII fame
61 Slowly permeate
65 Bighorn's mom

10 Brief Statements

by Alice Walker
Edited by Timothy E. Parker

Copyright © 2010 Universal Uclick

ACROSS

1 It may be compact
5 Whole ball of wax (with "from")
9 Inquires
13 Cookie jar denizen, perhaps
14 Show validity
15 Word with "gift" or "thrift"
16 Pond swimming duck
17 Parcels of earth
18 Have feelings
19 Short-lived success
22 New hire
24 Upturned
25 Like a has-been (with 41-Across)
29 Islamic princes
30 Hamlet, for one
31 "Mystery!" channel
34 ___ serif
35 Rock opera by The Who
37 Something to raise
38 Celebrated twin
39 Burt's wife, once

40 Body trunk
41 See 25-Across
44 It's bound to show the way
47 Ozzie and Harriet, e.g.
48 Terse
52 Feudal serf, e.g.
53 Pauline's problem
54 Citrus fruit
57 Sea eagle
58 Ranks contestants
59 Organic compound
60 Swallow flat
61 Leg up
62 Exclamation of the work-weary

DOWN
1 Small circle
2 Blood-pressure raiser
3 Oceangoing
4 Coal miners
5 Like a frightened cat's back
6 Spelling or Amos
7 Baker's pride
8 Gusto
9 Go to a higher level
10 Mold or fashion
11 Islamic text (Var.)
12 Pass bills
14 Former Toyota model
20 Wee workers
21 Fine-tune
22 Nearby objects
23 Put on a new crew
26 Word on a ticket
27 Orange food

28 "____ takers?"
31 Mindlessly repeating
32 Buffalo kin
33 Bamboozles
35 Cargo measure
36 Small cardinal
37 Breastplate
39 In need of a map
40 Metalware
41 January birthstone
42 Type of kick, in football
43 Whimpers
44 Vail rival
45 Yonder
46 Batty-sounding birds
49 Cathedral area
50 It can be pressing
51 Small amount
55 Miss Piggy's pronoun
56 Mischievous little creature

by Leana Bloom
Edited by Timothy E. Parker

ACROSS

1 Stereotypical hobo fare
5 There's no accounting for it
10 Turkish topper
13 ___ Major
14 Greek alphabet starters
16 George's musical brother
17 Nature personified
19 Music genre
20 Breakfast of centurions?
21 Courage
22 Cheer for the matador
24 Incriminate falsely
26 Owing payments
30 Negligent
32 Clinging part of a climbing plant
33 Start to dominate?
34 Cartridge holder
35 Mortar rounds, e.g.
36 Form of English
39 Valuable weasels
42 Create a dart, e.g.
43 ___ mater (brain membrane)

45 Mighty long time
46 Type of reaction
48 Pizza sauce enhancer
50 Properly clothed
53 Put into a new order
55 Has down pat
57 Butting bighorn
58 Molded, frozen dessert
60 By way of
61 Slugging stat
63 A bit too serious
66 Standard product, once
67 40th U.S. president
68 Pot additive
69 Exclamation of wonder
70 Improve, as a text
71 Angler's prize, sometimes

DOWN
1 Large Japanese guys
2 Common-law action to recover damages
3 Mansion and grounds
4 Half a trumpet's sound
5 Poi source
6 Joan's "Dynasty" role
7 New World colonizer
8 Imperil
9 Gormandize, e.g.
10 Combat supplies
11 Historic time
12 Laser gun sound effect
15 Like many a cold sheep
18 Darth Vader's dominion
23 "___ and the Swan" (Yeats)

25 Guy who cries foul
27 Fail to keep a promise
28 Icy cover
29 Give me a brake?
31 Star close to Venus?
34 Word with "ten" or "hair"
36 Olfactory perception
37 Tackle box item
38 Without much cheer
40 Night light
41 Chump
44 Indian tourist site
47 Pin number?
49 Museum suit
50 Abase
51 Series of repeated Catholic prayers
52 Ironic turns
54 Eat more than one's fill
56 Eats more than one's fill
59 Boston or Chicago, e.g.
61 Scottish hero Roy
62 Short life story?
64 Rock singer Bobby
65 Capture a crook

12 Letter-Perfect

by Mark Milhet
Edited by Timothy E. Parker

Copyright © 2010 Universal Uclick

ACROSS

1 Member of the common class
6 Withhold wages from
10 Heron cousin
14 Less experienced
15 First name in scat
16 "Bringing Up Father" girl
17 Lend ___ (pay close attention)
18 Not having much fat
19 Loretta's "M*A*S*H" co-star
20 Behave, letter-perfectly
23 Fury
24 "___ to you, buddy!"
25 End of a dry spell
28 Victorian, for one
31 Buffet selections, often
35 Barley fibers, e.g.
36 Finished
38 Part of the Fertile Crescent
39 Slap the cuffs on

40 Tic-tac-toe plays, letter-perfectly
42 Treat leather
43 Bleak, in verse
45 They're cut by dancers
46 Locate
47 Sketch over
49 Ring around the collar?
50 Swing a scythe
51 Tournament freebies
53 "Before" of yore
55 Complete a contract, letter-perfectly
63 Brief notice in passing
64 Popular summer destination
65 Place for a Chicago touchdown?
66 Glittering vein
67 Popular cookie brand
68 Fracas
69 Satyric stare
70 Spider's home
71 Scrooge's expression

DOWN
1 Soho stroller
2 One-time Delhi queen
3 "A Prayer for ___ Meany"
4 Introductions
5 Kind of message
6 Take-out order?
7 Picadors' praise
8 Puts palms together
9 Dorothy's home
10 In a silly manner
11 Font property, sometimes
12 Modern Mesopotamia
13 Word with "souci" or "serif"
21 Requisites
22 Accrue
25 Abbreviated vacation goal, letter-perfectly
26 Hardly oblivious
27 Under cover
29 Sound in the jungle
30 Make void
32 Shaw of swing
33 Paul Anka's first hit
34 Wall St. "500," letter-perfectly
37 Defeat by a hair
40 They give the inside picture
41 Willow for wicker
44 Dispute settler
46 Add ice, as to an old drink
48 It can be concealed
52 Midnight rumble
54 Suite things
55 Kewpie, e.g.
56 Clarinet cousin
57 Almanac topic
58 The Johns we don't know
59 Congeal
60 Retail lure
61 Bat's beginning
62 Soothsayer

13 Ride Along

by Lucky Barrett
Edited by Timothy E. Parker

ACROSS

1 Word introducing Johnny
6 Greasy spoon fare
10 Sidney Poitier, e.g.
14 Counting everything
15 Little pat on your buns?
16 Basilica center
17 Certain carriage
19 "Rag Mop" brothers
20 One on a golf scorecard
21 Shoulder protection
22 Proposals
24 West End attraction
26 Run at the mouth
27 Pink lady ingredient
28 Checkers, across the Atlantic
31 Wimps' opposites
34 Buck or Bailey
35 Alleged paranormalist Geller
36 Outback creatures
37 Sentimental one
38 Industrial-strength air?

39 Need nursing
40 Church parts, perhaps
41 Perception factor
42 One with the shivers, e.g.
44 Bonnet invader
45 Mah-jongg equipment
46 Some sugar containers
50 Head of a pen
52 He hit 66 homers in 1998
53 Miss Piggy's pronoun
54 "Good heavens!"
55 Nintendo hit
58 Billiard cushion
59 Clarinet cousin
60 Digested
61 Seabird
62 Some are prime
63 Color changers

DOWN
1 Part of a drum kit, informally
2 Father of Methuselah
3 Public performance (with "show")
4 Two-time U.S. Open winner Ernie
5 Rose late
6 Nomadic group
7 Old-style "Bummer!"
8 Put in stitches
9 Like some degrees
10 Bewildered
11 Mound in the Sahara?
12 Done
13 "Good" or "bad" ending

18 Sock-mender's oath?
23 Ball for the fans
25 Awfully long time
26 Old-fashioned exclamations
28 Postpone an action
29 Run without rushing
30 Audible breath
31 What mobsters pack?
32 Arab potentate
33 Frankie Laine hit of 1949
34 Does modeling work
37 Magnificence
38 "___ and ye shall find"
40 Having the means
41 Less radioactive
43 Waistline
44 Statue part
46 Nudges
47 Be a drama queen
48 Photocopying need
49 Speaks without speaking
50 Existed
51 Lab media
52 One looking down on you?
56 ___-Wan Kenobi
57 Diane in "The Godfather"

14 Have a Blast

by James E. Buell
Edited by Timothy E. Parker

Copyright © 2010 Universal Uclick

ACROSS

1 Cookbook instruction
5 Irritation
9 Souvenir of the past
14 ___ of operation
15 100 centavos
16 Drama at La Scala
17 Have a blast!
19 Web destinations
20 High, rocky hill
21 It's found among needles
23 From head to foot
27 Room service decanters, e.g.
28 Italian liqueur
30 Dirty money
31 Word in a Hitchcock film title
32 Stored away
34 One-time stratospheric streaker
37 Carpenter and harvester
38 Actor Leary
39 Snorkel's pooch

\text{page 28}

40 Myrna of "The Thin Man"
41 Some night sounds
42 Golf great Sam
43 Kind of trigger
45 Broken off, musically
47 First Mets skipper Casey
50 Buildings with steeply pitched roofs
51 Pressured
53 Type of computer memory
54 Ahead of time
55 Have a blast!
60 First name in mascara
61 Bird of Old Rome
62 Licentious man
63 Tense (with "up")
64 Son of Eve
65 Provide with a hideout, perhaps

DOWN
1 It's headquartered in Munich
2 "That's awesome!"
3 Terse vow
4 Dancers' wear, sometimes
5 Apparition
6 Invoice word
7 "The jig ___!"
8 Debaters' need
9 Like cheeks, at times
10 Long and impressive
11 Have a blast!
12 Cara or Ryan
13 Detective's assignments

18 Vatican honchos
22 Locks may hide them
23 Junta
24 Organic acid form
25 Have a blast!
26 Anesthetic liquid
29 Sow sounds
33 Western scene
35 Union member
36 Hoo-has
38 Tested one's courage
39 Being shot
41 Filled with awe
42 "Beat it!"
44 Founder of the Shakers, in America
46 From the beginning
47 Streamlined
48 Display poor sportsmanship, in a way
49 ___ de Zamora, Argentina
52 Basilica center
56 "Caboodle" partner
57 Take the wrong way?
58 Lament
59 Thus far

15 Costs About a Grand

by Pepper Castling
Edited by Timothy E. Parker

ACROSS

1 Taxi or taxi driver
5 45 and 78, e.g.
9 Empty-headed
14 Symptom of malaria
15 "Brian's Song" star
16 Inflexible
17 Three grand things
20 Exordium, informally
21 "... ___ forgive our debtors"
22 King Kong's co-star
23 Passionate pair
25 ___ Lanka
27 It's grand
34 Plane's place
35 Spot for the masses?
36 Big D.C. lobbyist
37 Could be fine, could be graphic
38 No. cruncher
39 Service entrance location, sometimes
40 "Infant" ending

41 Feast with a roast pig
43 Excessively
45 Two grand things
48 Loop for 41-Across
49 Roman emperor
50 Animal advocate (Abbr.)
53 Unlikely to bite
56 Creator of a count
60 Three grand things
63 Correct a tire pull
64 Where to find most of us
65 Unpleasant thing to eat
66 On edge
67 Center of Miami
68 Sweethearts, once

DOWN
1 Traveler to Mecca (Var.)
2 "Son of ___!"
3 Rudely brief
4 They hold jingly things
5 Magnavox rival
6 Noted canal
7 Baseball legend Willie
8 April or November surprise
9 Kind of agent
10 Birdbrain
11 Lab gel
12 Columbian ship
13 Whirlpool
18 Terra ___
19 Hatchling homes
24 Commit a faux pas
26 "Diff'rent Strokes" actress
27 Waitress with Sam and Coach
28 Stage direction

29 Emulate a cat with milk
30 Restorative resort
31 Sluggish by nature
32 Doctorate exam hurdles
33 ___ a one (zilch)
34 Rare weather forecast
38 Reef in the Florida Keys, e.g.
39 Swear off
41 Director Spike
42 Military groups
43 Miner's quest
44 "Falstaff" composer
46 Loud metallic sounds
47 Result of iron deficiency, perhaps
50 Young oyster
51 Carpet thickness
52 Genesis slayer
54 Woeful word
55 Trapper John's post
57 Noted critic of capitalism
58 Lotion addition
59 Applies patches, e.g.
61 Undivided
62 Common requests for info

16 Say-So

Edited by Timothy E. Parker

ACROSS

1 Elephantine
5 Shoe part
11 Two in a billion?
14 Onerous concern
15 Eyetooth
16 "Norma ___"
17 Beginning of a solver's thought
19 Certain road runner
20 Cube with spots
21 Pick a card, say
22 Jackrabbit, actually
23 Most definite
26 Moon feature
28 Solver's thought (Part 2)
32 Slithery Egyptian
33 Run
34 Sail supports
37 First name in pharmaceutical giants
38 Many Eastern Europeans
42 Air current heading skyward

Copyright © 2010 Universal Uclick

45 Start for "colonial"
46 Solver's thought
(Part 3)
51 Renaissance rulers
of Florence
52 Grasslands
53 Hippies' quarters
54 Halloween persona
57 Populous city area,
slangily
58 Jack Horner's last
words
59 End of a solver's
thought
64 Serve that doesn't
count
65 Scold
66 ___ fixe
67 Whichever
68 Jackson or Johnson
69 Workout spots

DOWN
1 Ad ___
2 Family card game
3 "Goody, goody" candy
4 Observes
5 It has a chilling effect
6 Alliance est. in 1949
7 Make little cuts
8 Window shade?
9 Chang's brother
10 Word with "shooter"
or "soup"
11 Margarine, vis-a-vis
butter
12 Hardycompanion?
13 Like some winter weather

18 Of reduced degree
22 Shirley Booth role
23 Dupe's undoing
24 Star bear
25 Number for the show?
26 IRS calculator?
27 Tiresome routines
29 "Lulu" or "Norma"
30 Switching device
31 Windblown snow pile
35 Capital of Tunisia
36 Done on ___
(without contract)
39 Disease-fighting
protein
40 Shrimp discard
41 Part of Buck's trilogy
43 Motorist's crime,
briefly
44 Highest part
46 High-jumping
antelope
47 Mariners
48 Three-legged calf, e.g.
49 Oversupply
50 Insect with pincers
54 It can be rounded up
55 Winged
56 Yard portal
59 Letters of indecision,
on a schedule
60 She lays around the
farm
61 Use needle and thread
62 Sleep stage
63 ___ Plaines, Illinois

17 Questions, Questions

by Turner Givens
Edited by Timothy E. Parker

ACROSS

1 That alternative?
5 Pursue wild geese?
10 Slimy sci-fi menace
14 Ridge of sand
15 Type of ship
16 Like the cream of the crop
17 Apply, in a way (with "on")
18 Like some nail polish
19 "Follow me!" slangily
20 Tasty zoo
23 Parabolic trajectory
24 Much-used pencil
25 "Spring forward" letters
28 Realtor's sign of success
31 Footless
35 At the summit
37 Start of an explanation, perhaps
39 Singer/judge Abdul
40 Carrot patch, e.g.
43 Cockamamy

44 French town of WWII fame

45 It has two black suits

46 Medicating

48 Reach across

50 It's often blue

51 Amos or Spelling

53 Poetic pasture

55 What a geologist makes at the bank?

62 Setting in Haydn's "The Creation"

63 Mover's challenge

64 Osmatic stimulant

66 College book

67 Some continental currency

68 Time for a break, often

69 Studio structures

70 Relative of the salmon

71 Big game?

DOWN

1 QB successes

2 Fad hoop

3 Words before "instant"

4 Art photo shade

5 Classic drink

6 Faith in country?

7 One of the acting Baldwins

8 Blackens

9 Novel flubs

10 Rim holder

11 Capital of Togo

12 ___ about (circa)

13 Cartwright and Franklin

21 Wifey (with "the")

22 Tea serving, in Britain

25 King of psalmists

26 Dictation taker, once

27 Roman wraps

29 Some tennis shots

30 Not exactly Einsteins

32 Ranch visitors

33 Smart guy

34 Gangling

36 Some fasters

38 Edible seaweed

41 Highest natural adult male voice

42 Crossbar holder

47 Raisins' predecessors

49 New beginning?

52 Latin name for Troy

54 In harmony

55 N.Y. team

56 ___ fixe (obsession)

57 On deck

58 Truth alternative

59 Chemical compound

60 Object of devotion

61 Commandeered

65 They may administer IVs

ACROSS

1 Blacken, as barbecue fare
5 On the ball
10 Boat launch
14 Actor Alan of "Gilligan's Island"
15 It needs a good paddling
16 Pennsylvania lake port
17 "Ghostbusters" director Reitman
18 Composer Bruckner
19 Cinco de Mayo snack, perhaps
20 Card game for textile workers?
22 Word with "blight" or "guerrilla"
23 Crossing medium
24 Verb form for Virgil
26 Kind of club or column
33 Artistic touches
36 Potential progeny
37 Severe trial

38 Strange sighting
39 Figures in Hinduism
41 Willfully go downhill
42 Reach one's destination
44 Browning's "before"
45 Kind of son or daughter
46 It's falling down, in song
49 Venetian farewell
50 Outmoded
54 It's usually dressed before eaten
57 Conflict won by a horse
61 Olfactory nerve stimulator
62 Unwavering look
63 Dove shelter
64 Long-lasting hostilities
65 Tiny amounts
66 Julia's brother
67 Industrious six-footers
68 Silvery food fish
69 Telegraphed

DOWN
1 Marx born Leonard
2 Bad thing to cause
3 Having winglike extensions
4 Blockbuster's business
5 Use a certain office machine
6 Be suspended
7 Disapproving
8 "Boys Town" star
9 Part of it may be felt
10 Secondhand tire
11 Cairo league

12 Sparkly rock substance
13 Lowly laborer
21 Name in the Beatles' inner circle
22 Patrons
25 Buttressed (with "up")
27 Nine-day series of Catholic prayers
28 Zsa Zsa's sister
29 Word to a gator?
30 Relaxation partner
31 Third-base coach's sign, sometimes
32 Piece of paper
33 Twofold in nature
34 Crew cut's opposite
35 Brought forth
39 Bypass
40 Jackie O's spouse
43 Airport check-in essentials
45 Deadly meetings?
47 Baby part
48 Univ. admission criterion
51 Used inelegant language
52 Ellington's "___ Doll"
53 Upright, as posture
54 Chesterfield, for one
55 Oil port
56 Ill-mannered boor
58 Bank posting
59 Like gentlemen's agreements
60 Bit of banter
62 Venus, to Serena

19 Start Me Up

by Thomas Lucas
Edited by Timothy E. Parker

Copyright © 2010 Universal Uclick

ACROSS

1 Spread outward
6 "… your goodness ___ a morning cloud" (Hosea)
10 Sackcloth material, perhaps
14 Large ocean vessel
15 Juicer refuse
16 Good opponent
17 Western
18 Captain Hook's assistant
19 Ballistics, dynamic or lite starter
20 Three eye openers?
23 Hot time in Paris
24 Lined up (with "in")
25 "Dallas" character
28 Surmounting
31 Make a mistake
35 Detroit River's destination
37 "Your turn," in radiospeak
39 Margin of victory at the track, perhaps

40 Three cold fronts?
43 Any of various willows
44 Father figures
45 Blind piece
46 Covert
48 "Uh-uh"
50 Kind of dog
51 "An Inconvenient Truth" star
53 New Haven collegian
55 Three kick starts?
63 Forsaken
64 It's usually screwed up
65 Skip a syllable, e.g.
66 DeMille specialty
67 Peak of perfection
68 Begin, as winter
69 Refuse to admit
70 "___ we forget"
71 Way the wind blows

DOWN
1 Complete failure
2 One with no capacity for veracity
3 Oppositionist
4 Parish official
5 Published mistakes
6 Dixit lead-in
7 Type of wrestler
8 "The Downeaster ___" (Billy Joel song)
9 Weapons, long ago
10 Concerns for sailors and pilots
11 Unceasingly
12 Tract of wet ground
13 Walk heavily

21 Wyoming mountain range
22 First name in strikeouts
25 River to the Rio Grande
26 Cropped up
27 Imitate
29 Poet of Rome's Golden Age
30 Praline ingredient, often
32 Certain water containers
33 Commonplace
34 Trivial
36 Hospital sign
38 Change the decor of
41 Three-part cookies
42 Colorado ski resort
47 Kind of ceremony
49 Most senior
52 Draw out
54 Good-for-nothing
55 Ran in fear
56 Piece of rodeo gear
57 Role for Julia
58 Trees in an O'Neill title
59 Aid in crime
60 Ceremonial act
61 Thor's dad
62 Hang in the balance

by Casey Rumblach
Edited by Timothy E. Parker

ACROSS

1 Certain tunics
5 Pound of flesh
9 Mental picture, e.g.
14 Lead-in for "graph"
15 Manipulative one
16 Nail-___ (tense situation)
17 Oft-used Latin abbreviation
18 Org. with eligibility rules
19 Course intro?
20 Of lesser importance
22 Some basketball game highlights
23 Coward of England
24 Leave it, editorially
26 Prohibit
29 River duck
31 Breakfast order, perhaps
35 It's larger than Lincoln
37 Old Soviet news agency
39 63,360 inches
40 Puerto ___
41 Concession stand offerings

42 Lily Pons specialty
43 Stocking shade, sometimes
44 Nonkosher
45 Small flying insects
46 Lead-in for Madre or Leone
48 Jules Verne character
50 "Dick and Jane" verb
51 Actress Lollobrigida
53 Swarm
55 Chew out
58 Does some woolgathering
63 Vatican-related
64 Certain Japanese people
65 "Dagnabbit"
66 Be the life of the party
67 March fifteenth, to Caesar
68 Crowning point
69 In disarray
70 Pro ___ (proportionate)
71 Rich soil

DOWN
1 Natural mimics
2 Type of shift
3 Bric-a-___
4 Where to make waves?
5 Hogan movie role
6 It'll give you a lift
7 One of a storied threesome
8 Airline seat parts
9 Word in footnotes
10 Revolutionary War figure
11 Abbr. on a business envelope, perhaps
12 Carnival oddball
13 Plays a wrong note, e.g.
21 "___ creature was stirring..."
25 Fail to fall asleep, in a way
26 Tiresome ones
27 Latin friends
28 Mother-of-pearl
30 Heavily burdened
32 Turkish money units
33 Social creme de la creme
34 Badger
36 Primitive timepiece
38 Trapeze artist's security
41 Spider-Man creator Lee
45 "Movie" or "party" attachment
47 Director Scott
49 Snake-haired woman of myth
52 Noted fighter of oil fires
54 Olympian's quest
55 Some junk mail
56 "And it ___ to pass..."
57 Major musical composition
59 Noted opera
60 With the bow, in music
61 Nursery word
62 Cherry part

by James E. Buell
Edited by Timothy E. Parker

Copyright © 2010 Universal Uclick

ACROSS

1 She followed Eleanor
5 Conserve
9 Emcee with White
14 Way out
15 Throw in the towel
16 Decorate
17 Dey's revolving tray?
19 Sheet of print
20 Aviator Earhart
21 It was given to you
23 Give permission
24 Screwed up
26 Antiknock fluids
28 Noted horn blower
31 Flexible ___ sled
32 Feeling poorly
33 Conventions
35 Propels a wherry
38 Swindles
40 Just a bit
41 Like the color purple
42 Author Uris
43 Defunct Chrysler marque

45 Epoch
46 They were used
for many calls
48 Military force, once
50 Orville Wright's city
of birth
52 Seat weaver, of a sort
53 Cola mixer
54 Jazz plays there
56 Candied
60 Yikes!
62 Pesci's sandwich?
64 High spot for eggs
65 Mallet game
66 Molten spew
67 Salon fixture
68 There's one under
67-Across
69 They were once
together

DOWN
1 Lugosi of film
2 Student stressor
3 Junior or jumbo, e.g.
4 Salon fixture or employee
5 Certain shapes
6 Salzburg's nation, briefly
7 Delicious dish
8 Volcano near Messina
9 It's supposed to come first
10 Commotion
11 Ebert in a merry mood?
12 Mischievous spirit in
"The Tempest"
13 Pine feature
18 Dog Star
22 Gibson and Torme

25 Lifts, as spirits
27 This place
28 Kind of scout
29 Hand cream enhancer
30 What Moore may put
on her bar tab?
31 Felt hat
34 Laughing matter?
36 Lovesome
37 Assassin's order
39 Purl partner
41 Arrived on horseback
43 It might be created by
accident
44 Slangy Andrew
Jackson
47 Skilled housecat
49 Patterned sock
50 Great fear
51 When you use it,
it's boring
52 Daphnis' lover
55 Dangerous Middle
Easterners
57 Comet competitor
58 Wander about
59 Votes in favor
61 It may be cast
63 Pay stub?

by Lester Mapple
Edited by Timothy E. Parker

ACROSS

1 Resigner of October 10, 1973
6 Famous fabler
11 "It's freezing!"
14 Dill swill
15 Sri ___
16 Tolstoy's first
17 Fruity loaf
19 Actress Gardner
20 Asner's cheese choice?
21 Chicago political name
22 Desert Storm missile
23 Vein pursuit?
25 Second-chance exams
27 Ribbed cover
32 Drab partner
33 Cigarette stat
34 Turns sharply
36 Keep ___ to the ground
39 Worship
41 Command to a horse
42 European nation
43 Axman, e.g.

44 "Don't ___ the
   small stuff!"
46 Born as
47 Untouchable lawman
49 Backs a candidate
51 Paper pads
54 Anger
55 Stouts, e.g.
56 Uplift
59 No-see-um
63 Mass. school
64 Meaty wrap
66 Guinea pig, often
67 Paris landmark (with "L)
68 Not on deck
69 Random choice
70 Financier John Jacob
71 Wish list entries

DOWN
1 Ex of Cugie
2 Commencement
   honoree, briefly
3 A historic ship
4 Win the heart of
5 Harmless cyst
6 ___ Longa (birthplace of
   Romulus and Remus)
7 British peer
8 Scornful smile
9 Authorized
10 Toad's stool?
11 Feijoada ingredients
12 Vaudeville production
13 Many have shoulders
18 Fred Astaire's sister
22 Louisiana athlete
24 Kind of discrimination

26 Turncoat
27 State of the
   union address
28 Crafted
29 Baked dessert
30 Calf locales
31 "___ having fun yet?"
35 "No man hath ___
   God at any time"
   (John 1:18)
37 Away from the wind
38 Bread choices
40 Emulates a toper
45 "Cheerio!"
48 Prepares in a teapot
50 Feel sorry about
51 Florida bay
52 It's out of this world
53 Winter driving hazard
57 Spheroid hairdo
58 Lifting device
60 Khartoum river
61 Tiny particle
62 Expensive car trips
64 It'll put the squeeze
   on you
65 Box score stat

by Leana Bloom
Edited by Timothy E. Parker

ACROSS

1 Feel sore
5 Carp relative
9 In the boondocks, e.g.
14 Seafood item
15 Many a Norwegian king
16 Standing-foot link
17 Introduce opposition
20 "To the max" indicator
21 Maui shindig
22 Classic TV series set
  in Calverton
23 He is holy, to many
25 "Keen!"
27 Polo competitor
29 Going on and on and…
33 Make an effort
37 As well
38 Canal of renown
39 Blip on a polygraph
40 School established
  in 1440
41 2 oz., e.g.
42 Come to ruin

46 Classic U-boat film
48 "The Little Red Hen" denial
49 Lucy's best friend
51 Family reunion activity
55 Number five iron
58 Landers and others
60 Contend
61 Rise to preeminence
64 Leavening agent
65 Culinary directive
66 They need refinement
67 ___ Domingo
68 Like a busy mechanic's rags
69 Literary governess Jane

DOWN
1 "Green ___" (classic sitcom)
2 Necklace fastener
3 Dominican Republic's neighbor
4 Maximum limits?
5 Swindle
6 Goya's "The Duchess of ___"
7 Like some Louisianan cuisine
8 Woman in a garden
9 Pitcher's cuff
10 Homophony
11 Outback leapers, briefly
12 MMVII and others
13 ___-majeste
18 Flower girl Doolittle
19 ___ Boothe Luce

24 Ceremonial act
26 Squeeze beside
28 Thin, as a solvent
30 "Leave ___ Beaver"
31 Sheltered and secluded place
32 Neither here nor there
33 Cause of painter's colic
34 "The Madwoman of Chaillot" role
35 Looks great on
36 Tiny bite
40 Send off, as broadcast waves
42 Became involved with
43 Expressed wonderment, in a way
44 What "Keep out!" means
45 Put away for a rainy day
47 Urgent prompting
50 Christine of "Chicago Hope"
52 Coast or tower
53 Frisco gridder
54 Gaggle members
55 Aaron contemporary
56 Between ports
57 Observatories do it
59 Lunar Armstrong
62 General one can take out?
63 Caviar

24 Round We Go

by Emery Glasso
Edited by Timothy E. Parker

ACROSS

1 Disney elephant
6 Caribbean Eden
11 Insult, slangily
14 Newton of gravity fame
15 Kingdom
16 Picnic scurrier
17 Nature personified
19 Attachment to ox or roads
20 Heavy metal
21 Barbara's role on "Dallas"
23 Snore
27 "The Human Comedy" novelist
29 Takes into one's family
30 Arises unexpectedly
31 Arctic floaters
32 Blow one's top
33 It was dropped in the '60s
36 "Deck the Halls" syllables
37 Dizzying painting movement

38 Between the lines, in baseball
39 Ancient times, in ancient times
40 Narrow openings
41 New York's ___ Island
42 Jukebox verb
44 Record jacket, e.g.
45 Sound systems
47 Kitchen appliance
48 Welsh canine
49 Monopoly token
50 William Tell's canton
51 Movie award since 1944
58 Common Father's Day gift
59 Shoe-repair shop stock
60 Ghastly strange
61 Bro counterpart
62 Gives an effort
63 Interior designer's doing

DOWN
1 Lacking brightness
2 Wartime entertainers
3 Floor covering
4 Kin of phooey
5 Spotted wildcats
6 Localities
7 Crack a book
8 Short-lived Middle Eastern federation (Abbr.)
9 Sandwich initials
10 Emily Dickinson's Massachusetts birthplace
11 Lois Lane's employer (with "The")

12 "Gunga Din" setting
13 Dutch painter Jan
18 Rules' partners, briefly
22 Baseball legend Gehrig
23 Weasel cousin
24 "Let's Make ___"
25 October sports event
26 Org. for Annika Sorenstam
27 Worsens, as relations
28 Meeting with an M.D.
30 Engine maker ___ & Whitney
32 Extended narratives
34 Colander kin
35 Laundry machine
37 Ersatz butter
38 Contenders
40 Adroitness in using the hands
41 Sounded like a trolley?
43 Small bit of work
44 Any time now
45 Rabbits' tails, e.g.
46 Shinto temple gateway
47 Plait of hair
49 Not up to much
52 "___ the ramparts…"
53 Hawaiian welcome token
54 "Enter the Dragon" star Bruce
55 "The Lord of the Rings" monster
56 Life story, for short
57 Occupational suffix

by Turner Givens
Edited by Timothy E. Parker

Copyright © 2010 Universal Uclick

ACROSS

1 Puts suddenly, as a question
5 Sixth-day creation
9 Martin or Lawrence
14 It could provide a pat on the buns
15 Solemn observance, e.g.
16 Anecdotes
17 Air
18 Grand poetry
19 It's valuable
20 North and south, e.g.
23 Agitate
24 Comically off-the-wall
25 Expected to arrive
28 Assorted
30 Zebra kin
33 Da Gama destination
35 Took the bait
36 One in an old empire
37 Hardly a warm welcome
41 Bloodsucking arachnid

42 "So, there you are!"
43 Disputed matter
44 Bright, as a pupil
45 Unseen troublemaker
48 Make a wrong choice, e.g.
49 Cool off like a boxer
50 Rainfall measurement
52 Take a break
58 "___ Attraction" (1987)
59 Lead, for one
60 Computer image
61 Fanny of the Ziegfeld Follies
62 "___ Rhythm"
63 "Buzz off!"
64 Like some triggerfingers
65 Frightens
66 Grant's landmark

DOWN
1 Ceremonial elegance
2 Salmagundi, e.g.
3 Sunburn aftermath
4 Submarine tracker
5 Nipple ring
6 Big or Little in the sky
7 Resting on
8 One era
9 Sloppy eaters' problems
10 Scrumptious
11 Word in a conditional statement, perhaps
12 Vivid twosome
13 Md. setting
21 Be in competition with
22 Recipe direction, sometimes

25 Forma pronounce-ments
26 Not very cool
27 ___ of Nantes, 1598
29 Type of iron girder
30 Absinthe flavoring
31 Scrub strenuously
32 More sound
34 Variety
36 Part of FWIW
38 Adventurer's inventory
39 Pretentious speech
40 Small amount
45 Ship's kitchen
46 Stay off the radar
47 Some blowups
49 Hunt illegally
51 Yegg's job
52 Option for golfers
53 Involving the ear
54 NASA scratch
55 Kind of cardiogram
56 Appear imminent
57 Highbrow
58 Department of Justice div.

26 Camera-Ready

by Henry Quarters
Edited by Timothy E. Parker

Copyright © 2010 Universal Uclick

ACROSS

1 Civil rights activist Parks
5 Nursery rhyme Jack
10 What to do "in the name of love"
14 Cartel since 1960
15 Island in the Netherlands Antilles
16 "One More Night" singer Collins
17 Ethiopian slave of opera
18 Cuban VIP
19 Slippery and slithery
20 Huddle outcomes?
23 Feebleness
24 Secret supply
27 Pewter containing about 80 percent tin
28 Rail transport, perhaps
31 Island instrument, for short
32 Brit's raincoat
34 Tex-Mex dish
35 Projecting edge
36 Like a bad photographer's subject?

40 "Human Concretion" artist
41 Well-informed
42 Fish story suffix?
43 Smoker's amassment
44 Buddhist shrine
45 Curative place
47 Turns sharply
49 Flowering shrubs
53 What the marksman took at midnight? (with "a")
57 It has a cream center
59 Revere
60 Major or minor constellation
61 They're made only at home
62 Red Cross volunteer
63 Stop the bleeding
64 Network of nerves, e.g.
65 Aspen area
66 Daly of the stage

DOWN
1 Meat cut
2 State as an opinion
3 Enclosed automobile
4 Mexican cruise port
5 Kind of zone
6 Quite expensive (Var.)
7 Fashion designer Gernreich
8 Vigoda and Lincoln
9 Anklebones
10 Exhausted
11 Book of synonyms
12 It eases friction

13 Tissue layer, e.g.
21 Six-sided game piece
22 Containing element number 76
25 Evade
26 Complex, red organic pigment
28 Pointed-out direction
29 At fruition
30 The Greatest
32 Subway artwork, e.g.
33 Currently
34 Bloke
36 Cereal ingredients
37 String bean's opposite
38 Tango requirement
39 Weeping conduit
45 Heavenly body shape
46 Thanksgiving dessert
48 A question of possession
49 Sharpening strap
50 With time to spare
51 Insurance-scamming crime
52 It has wheels on its heel
54 Small amounts
55 False god
56 Forbidden action
57 Canadian hockey legend
58 Have regrets

Copyright © 2010 Universal Uclick

ACROSS

1 Rounded end of a church
5 Sportscast tidbit
9 Wrapped up
13 Shaving aid
14 Steno's goof
15 Spanish flick
16 Choice many face
19 Looks perfect on
20 Greek letter
21 Give great pleasure to
22 Otherwise called (Abbr.)
23 Sweet-smelling necklace
24 Crayola user
26 Choice many face
29 Places bets
30 Big commotions
31 Short smoke?
34 Exercise judgment
35 On the wagon
37 Pueblo Indian
38 Trip or slip, e.g.
39 Broad, thick piece

40 Backs, anatomically
41 Choice many face
44 Surgical implements
47 "How soothing!"
48 Newt wannabe
49 It may be heard coming and going
50 Feel malaise
51 Significant times
52 Choice many face
56 Islamic prayer leader
57 Sound made by a swinger?
58 Speak angrily
59 Thumb condition?
60 Tennyson's title
61 "Let ___!" (advice to the obsessed)

DOWN
1 Boer
2 Inferior rhymer
3 Gives under a load
4 Bird raised for its red meat
5 Kind of electricity
6 Banks, formerly of the runway
7 Mil. address
8 Rocky peak
9 Yellow and black cat
10 Bishop's assistant
11 Maternally related
12 Give someone the business?
17 Masher's look
18 Sub stations
19 Pretense

23 Part of LAX
24 Relinquish
25 Permeating quality
27 Fashion's bottom line?
28 Temple official
31 Gaining control over, in a way
32 By the fact itself
33 Some fairy tale characters
35 Coin destination, sometimes
36 Wilkes' plantation Twelve ___
37 Biblical mount where Aaron was buried
39 Stain or smudge
40 Homer Simpson expletive
41 Crook's plan, e.g.
42 Got just right
43 Lavish celebration
44 ___ lazuli
45 Mission in San Antonio
46 Without face value, as stock
50 One who sincerely flatters?
51 French state
53 Screech producer
54 Letter after pi
55 Mr. in Bombay

28 Box Office Poison

by Thomas Lucas
Edited by Timothy E. Parker

ACROSS

1 Opposite of c.o.d.
4 Viking reading
8 Deli counter order, perhaps
14 Thole filler
15 Created a sketch
16 Having wings
17 One of every two hurricanes
18 Abyss
19 Posts on the stairs
20 Deli counter order, perhaps
23 Settle (into)
24 Festive occasion
25 Joie de vivre
29 Lithesome
31 Corporate routine
34 Emphatic ending (Var.)
35 "It's ___ the other!"
37 Ante matter?
38 It creates a big splash
41 Burier of Pompeii
44 Hoity-___

45 Multicolored pattern
49 "Uncle Vanya" playwright
51 Pudding-like dessert
52 Popular lunch salad
53 Lake, city or canal
56 "Dial ___ Murder"
57 It was first tested in 1952
61 Churchill's successor and predecessor
64 Recipe direction
65 Portuguese king
66 Repairman's reading
67 For, how or what ending
68 Soldier's fare, for short
69 Instruments with teakwood necks
70 Feudal peasant
71 Man of Steel monogram

DOWN
1 Call one's own
2 Shah's surname
3 "An American Tragedy" writer
4 Borderline
5 Hard worker at boring tasks
6 Geological formation
7 Not just bad
8 Went down like a cement block
9 Toward one side of a ship
10 Someone on the defense, perhaps
11 "Thanks, I already ___"
12 Cartoon voice Blanc

13 Proofs of age
21 Paparazzi's quarry, briefly
22 Make more subtle
26 Part of some college courses
27 Powerful heart
28 Angler's entangler
30 Gum attachments
32 Cyberspace initials
33 Prefix with sphere
35 Musical based on Dickens
36 Gotham paper (Abbr.)
39 London restaurant feature
40 Weight that sounds like a fruit
41 Step into character
42 Moo ___ pork
43 She may feel cooped up
46 Words preceding a personal preference
47 Chemically related compounds
48 Bowlers
50 Black Russian ingredient
51 More self-effacing
54 Judicial gowns
55 "___ at the office!"
58 Time for a revolution?
59 Shannon and Monte
60 Type of ball
61 Pre-noon hrs.
62 Mai ___ cocktail
63 You'll have a blast with it

29 Guys' Names

by Eugene Newman
Edited by Timothy E. Parker

Copyright © 2010 Universal Uclick

ACROSS

1 Lover's keepsake, perhaps
6 Babushka, e.g.
11 Zodiac symbol
14 Therefore
15 International court site (with "The")
16 Bravo kin
17 Good name for an electrician?
19 Salon preparation, perhaps
20 Debatable
21 Highland dance
22 Sluggish
24 Cargo deck
26 Magazine fallout?
28 Plied a needle
31 One way or another
33 Colorful perennials
35 CEO, e.g.
36 Teeny bites
39 Zilch

40 "The Public Enemy" sound effect
43 Summer zodiac sign
44 Moolah
46 Pied Piper devotee
47 Indian sailor
49 Matterhorn vocalist
52 Elected
53 Circular saw part
55 It's useful in October
57 Sharp and bitter
58 Endings for pay and plug
60 Otherwise
64 Baseball's Ripken
65 Good name for a healthcare specialist?
68 Fashion monogram
69 Painkiller made by Bayer
70 Vaudeville production
71 Pig's home
72 1960 Everly Brothers tune
73 Utopias

DOWN

1 The other team
2 Renovate
3 Prefix with morph
4 They cut quite a swath
5 Wine adjective
6 Destroys files, in a way
7 Upkeep
8 Bars have one
9 Seek office
10 Charm believed to embody magcal powers
11 Good name for a flier?
12 Wide-eyed
13 Dissolves
18 You may bookmark it
23 Gas that's hard to ignore
25 Czech river
27 Himalayan country
28 Try out for "American Idol"
29 Clinton's canal
30 Good name for an inefficient efficiency expert?
32 Skunk cabbage shape
34 Asian garment (Var.)
37 Porridge legumes
38 Vexed
41 Beer hall orders
42 Small fastener
45 Lincoln's wife
48 Swerved
50 Fuel additive, perhaps
51 Like "The Godfather"
53 Noted parade sponsor
54 "With ___ of thousands!"
56 Type of tray
59 Units of money in Bulgaria
61 Wash
62 Told, as a tale
63 Watches
66 "Evil Woman" band
67 Before, poetically

by Timothy Winton
Edited by Timothy E. Parker

ACROSS

1 Wedding symbol
5 Louts
10 Show signs of life
14 Wavy lines, in comics
15 Be in competition with
16 Purplish brown
17 Armed Forces option
18 It's larger than Lincoln
19 Dorsal bones
20 Vestige
21 Knowledgeable
23 Certifiable, so to speak
25 Munchhausen and Ananias, for two
26 Tear maker
28 "Big deal!"
32 Tied the knot
34 Farmer's necessity
35 Ebenezer's expletive
38 Chronological brinks
39 Blank tapes?
41 Physics force measure

42 Its floor is wet
43 Work at a diner, e.g.
44 Part of a baseball's seam
46 Reference point
48 Phoenix origin
49 Hollywood treasure
52 Draw out
54 Like a simple task
58 "SOS" singers
61 Yule follower
62 Capital of Tibet
63 It's over your head
64 Without advantage or disadvantage
65 Pointed a bow, e.g.
66 One word of advice
67 Like a Granny Smith apple
68 Subdivision maps
69 "The ___ the limit!"

DOWN
1 Interest-bearing certificate
2 Month before Nisan
3 Original thought
4 Fabrics for sale
5 Jack broke it
6 English gobs
7 Geometric shape
8 "James and the Giant Peach" author
9 Eastern European
10 Medium contact?
11 City on the Arkansas River
12 More gelid

13 Is a bibliophile
22 Spirited self-assurance
24 Its root is itself
26 Has to return a favor, e.g.
27 Alpine snow field
29 Emulate Demosthenes
30 Is no longer?
31 Scurries
33 Precious
35 How officials do things?
36 Suffix for allow or annoy
37 Derisive laughs
40 Big truck
41 Scraps
43 Hospital unit
45 Sigma follower
46 Kind of scout
47 Afternoon trayful, perhaps
49 Merger of two quartets
50 The Hindu destroyer
51 Juice from a press
53 Groups of two
55 Delivery after a delivery?
56 Marlo's man
57 Tibetan holy man
59 Without much meat
60 Some times of the day, briefly

ACROSS

1 Electronics brand
5 Oahu adieu
10 Sharp pain
14 Melancholy instrument
15 Tend to final details
16 Kind of steak
17 Happy time for landlords
20 Convenience store convenience, perhaps
21 Primitive shelters
22 Minipicture, maybe
23 Stunted
24 He can't bear anyone
26 Support
29 The color of honey
30 Comb maker
33 Bit of evidence
34 DVD player button
35 Pool table success
36 Hinterland, e.g.
40 Half-picas
41 Hovering in the sky
42 Nuclear energy source

43 Firmament
44 Brown alternative
45 Type of bow
47 Top-of-the-line
48 Opposite of flushed
49 Boat on a lake, perhaps
52 Type of cotton
53 It's placed in a setting
56 It comes about every 100 years
60 Caramel-and-chocolate candy brand
61 Testimonial dinner, e.g.
62 Judicial document
63 Jump on the ice
64 Gossipy gal
65 Sound of pain

DOWN
1 Daybed of sorts
2 News item for a scrapbook, briefly
3 100, I.Q.-wise
4 One of two definitive responses
5 Check entry
6 Like some ideas
7 Puts an end to wavering
8 "Say what?"
9 Wild way to go
10 Carry out Old Testament justice, in a way
11 Vintners' vessels
12 Deserve a hand?
13 Thailand money
18 Consequently
19 Fungi caused by moisture
23 Two-colored

24 Organize, as an exhibit
25 Among other things
26 Pinnacles
27 Move stealthily, in a way
28 Producing foamy lather
29 Social blunder
30 Quarterback Favre
31 Transnational money units
32 Kind of aircraft
34 British city on the English Channel
37 Unemploy temporarily
38 Distinctive flair
39 Fabled underachiever
45 Word with ready or shy
46 ___ Bator, Mongolia
47 "___ and his money..."
48 Embroidered loop
49 Title word in a Doris Day song
50 Fort with a fortune
51 Like some rumors
52 Teller's partner
53 Maven
54 Norwegian navigator
55 Legend
57 "___ will be done"
58 Farmer's tool
59 Binary base

32 Let's Do Lunch

by Casey Rumblach
Edited by Timothy E. Parker

ACROSS

1 With the stroke of ___
5 Vasco da ___, Portuguese explorer
9 Texas landmark
14 Withering
15 They're found in pockets
16 Palindromic tales
17 They may hang around delis?
20 Swahili honorific
21 Israeli dances
22 Niger end?
23 Minister, slangily
25 It's all over the streets
26 Word with monkey or serpent
29 Clears, on a pay stub
31 Locale of a small stirrup
33 Enjoyment in cruelty
35 Member of the crow family
38 Chivalrous chaps
39 Card fit for royalty?
41 Aristide's former home

43 Advertise for new tenants
44 Chronic respiratory disease
46 Campaigned
47 Keeps company with
51 Opposite direction of a Hitchcock classic?
52 Sharp-penned Coulter
54 Steeped beverage
56 Historic Swiss canton
57 Take the wrong way?
59 Fistfight result, perhaps
61 Top-10 tune of 1966
65 Broadcasting warning
66 Buffo performance, perhaps
67 Representative symbol
68 Witches' brew creatures
69 Revolutionary Trotsky
70 Hems but doesn't haw

DOWN
1 Furnace waste container
2 Olive-gray flycatcher
3 Off-course
4 Fluorine neighbor in the periodic table
5 Score of zero
6 Flight board abbreviation
7 Dovetail
8 "It's worth ___!"
9 Young vegetable shoot
10 Passes on the track
11 Eligibility factor
12 Render imperfect
13 1940s spy grp.
18 Kind of dance or bride

19 Things that can be rolled over, for short
24 Cloudy, diffused matter
26 Results from bad acting?
27 Ultimate ending
28 Wake-up times, typically
30 Pseudonym surname, often
32 More plentiful
34 Outstanding issues?
36 Cel creators
37 Conspicuous success
39 It operates on wind power
40 Grid official
41 Is down with
42 Cousin of a zebra
45 From a fresh angle
48 Carol Burnett character
49 Poetic "until this time"
50 Alluring women
53 Type of spray
55 "So, there you are!"
57 Narrow aperture
58 Fly on a hook, to bass
60 Flower of one's eye?
61 Hither partner
62 Ending for ethyl
63 Partner of order
64 Brief outline of life and work

33 Go Forth and Multiply

by Lester Mapple
Edited by Timothy E. Parker

1	2	3	4	■	5	6	7	8	■	9	10	11	12	13

ACROSS

1 Cops' decoy
5 Metric measure
9 One way to be wanted
14 Spread out on a table?
15 Freedom from hardship
16 Stage platform
17 Contents of some tablets
20 Line providers
21 1/60 of a trillionth of a min.
22 Squirt
23 Stars have them, briefly
25 Contented murmurs
27 Science degree
30 Anatomical pouches
32 Chorus syllables, perhaps
36 Caesar's wings
38 Reveille opposite
40 Ancient Greek colony
41 Conflict beginning in 1337
44 Line of work
45 Cleansing bar
46 Suspend
47 Send water flying

49 Relaxed rejection
51 Word of support
52 Bedding item
54 It's lost at the gym
56 Travel over powder
59 Mishmash
61 Citizens can make it
65 Part of an epic film, perhaps
68 Dispense
69 Mexican family circle members
70 Hypnosis ender
71 Sounds from the hood?
72 Worst kind of loser
73 Tony Fifth Avenue store

DOWN
1 "___ creature was stirring …"
2 Sir Guinness
3 How to have a flat?
4 Winter treat
5 Idaho's nickname
6 Southdown male
7 In a New York minute
8 Bright group
9 "All in the Family" prop
10 Bad thing to be caught in
11 That special leader?
12 Presidential power
13 Formerly, formerly
18 Assns.
19 Result of an agreement
24 A bunch
26 Wade through mud

27 Money of Thailand
28 Drink undaintily
29 Artificial waterway
31 Secretly watch
33 Menachem's peace partner
34 Vine
35 Exasperation exclamation
37 Icelandic works
39 "___ Love" (Pacino film)
42 Does a director's job
43 It can be canned
48 First of two parts
50 They may hold pencils
53 Little League equipment
55 Kind of band
56 Union defier
57 Cabbagelike plant
58 "Robinson Crusoe" locale
60 Place for Reds and Browns
62 Sicilian province or its capital
63 Pierre's place (Abbr.)
64 Recipe amounts, briefly
66 It may be blown
67 Flat-ended instrument

by Tucker Mathis
Edited by Timothy E. Parker

ACROSS

1 Clock radio switch
5 Firm parts, briefly
10 Soldiers for old Dixie
14 Casa component
15 Uncovers
16 Floor measure
17 Commiserator's word
18 Have a life
19 Parental admonition
20 Fires
22 Hindu social group
23 Exploit
24 Ingrain
26 Adagio, allegro, etc.
30 "Ghost Story" novelist Peter
32 WWII maritime hazard
34 Garment edge
35 Hands-on classes
39 Cartoon Betty
40 Biblical peak
42 Cannes brainstorm
43 Cost to be dealt in

44 Direct extender
45 Seem
47 Hindu queens
50 Bone of contention
51 Baseball position
54 They might give you
   a jump-start
56 Some precious stones
57 Some acrobatic
   maneuvers
63 Prefix with freeze
64 Words with may
   or might
65 American prefix
66 Bissextile year
67 Hogs' homes
68 "___ ain't broke..."
69 Disrespect, in a way
70 Mae and Adam
71 Isn't a natural

DOWN
1 Posthaste, briefly
2 French Sudan, now
3 Bakery offering
4 Camouflage
5 Adam's son and others
6 Prepares to take off
7 Misstep
8 Emphatic agreement
9 Craft that once landed
   at Heathrow
10 They're seen in air
   traffic control towers
11 Notched and jagged
12 Dispositions
13 Surfeits
21 Birthday attire?

22 PC's brain
25 Cobra relative
26 Hefty instrument
27 Deep black, in poesy
28 Subject to debate
29 Office items
31 Storied bear
   contingent
33 Shoe finish
36 Orange and lime,
   for two
37 Bringer of wine
   and flowers
38 Withering
41 Job for an
   orthodontist
46 Edith, the "little
   sparrow"
48 Sounds of delight
49 Soft bag containing
   perfumed powder
51 Embers
52 Breathing irregularity
53 Bye-byes
55 Words sung after
   "You must remember
   this"
58 How some cars are
   sold
59 Installed, as carpet
60 Not a done deal
61 ___-dieu
   (kneeling bench)
62 Elbow benders
64 Milan-Turin direction

Copyright © 2010 Universal Uclick

ACROSS

1 Booted, e.g.
5 Old-fashioned tie
10 Lux. neighbor
14 Homeroom response
15 Picked out
16 State forcefully
17 Lot measurement
18 What trains travel on
19 Home video format, once
20 Lowlifes
23 Foundation for something

24 Ancient fable spinner
25 Light measures
28 Ave. relative
30 Opera solo
31 Site for some rites
33 Chapter in history
36 Inventor's goal
40 Remained unused
41 "The Rose" penner
42 Opening bet, in poker
43 Symphonic silence symbol
44 Disturbing sounds

46 Prefix meaning "bone"
49 Changdeok Palace site
51 Lucille Ball musical of '43
57 ___-TASS (Russian news agency)
58 Holiday numbers
59 "That makes sense"
60 Edible tuber of Polynesia
61 Bones once called cubiti
62 A tide
63 Flat sound
64 Personal histories
65 Like some basements

DOWN
1 Carpet type
2 "My ___!"
3 Snack since 1912
4 Freeloader
5 Unlike this clue
6 The voice of Lamb Chop
7 They have heads and tails
8 Artist Edvard Munch's home
9 Kind of pattern
10 Mollycoddled
11 Becomes equal (with "out")
12 Can
13 Perceive
21 Athletic supporter
22 Le ___, France
25 Castle basements, in some films

26 Fertilizer chemical
27 Burn protection
28 Heating measures
29 Start of some Spanish place names
31 Bit of Latin conjugation
32 Place to pick lemons?
33 Fish-eating shore birds
34 Ad sales rep's quote
35 Anthropoids
37 ___ newt (witch's ingredient)
38 Legal matter
39 It may help move aircraft
43 Backup rockets?
44 Cattle snares
45 Possession indication
46 Last writes?
47 Words with "an example" or "a goal"
48 1917 marked their end
49 Antique guns
50 Black key
52 "Movin' ___" ("The Jeffersons" theme)
53 "Return of the Jedi" character
54 Under sail
55 Stationery order, perhaps
56 Gilbert Grape portrayer Johnny

Copyright © 2010 Universal Uclick

ACROSS
1 Mantra chanter of note
5 Kind of shot
10 Many have little ones
14 Superior to
15 Helpful sort
16 What you might be as busy as
17 Contract part, often
19 Sullivan had a really big one
20 ___-neck (horse defect)
21 Nickname for Rocky's portrayer
22 Place for landlubbers
24 Piggery
25 Like most homes
27 Gossipmonger
30 Revved, as the engine
31 About intro
32 Job for the board?
33 "Witness" actor Lukas
37 Wrinkled fruit
38 They may roll off the production line

39 Christiania today
40 Reduction
41 Hands over
42 Kind of bog or moss
43 Natural in Vegas
45 They may be engaged
46 Like some checks
49 What may be bro kin?
50 Legally responsible
51 Comedian DeLuise
52 The hot saison
55 Film lioness
56 It may come in pads
60 Some pub servings
61 One-celled protozoan (Var.)
62 Abbreviated version
63 Shannon and Monte
64 They may be before your eyes
65 Current letters

DOWN
1 Deposit of valuable ore
2 State
3 Distribute
4 Type of studio
5 With a heavy heart
6 Easter flower
7 "The Last King of Scotland" subject Amin
8 One-time closer Robb
9 Enormousness
10 They bring on disappointment
11 Regard with loathing
12 Inventor of the steel plow
13 Darned it
18 Spanish 101 word
23 Joan of Arc title, for short
24 Fish with lines
25 Kind of optimism
26 Invisible
27 "___ better believe it!"
28 Civil or elec. expert
29 "___ contendere" (no contest plea)
30 Feel mournful
32 List extenders
34 Not on solid ground?
35 Having wings
36 Chronic imbibers
44 Former Indian P.M. Shastri
45 Ribbonlike, braided fabric
46 Appeal earnestly
47 Valley on the moon (Var.)
48 Flip-chart support
49 Some are kept behind bars
51 Liability
52 Impressive in scope
53 Serve up the drinks, e.g.
54 "Layla" singer Clapton
57 One whose chest is protected, briefly
58 Bloom in "The Producers"
59 "I ___ lineman for the county"

by Fred Jackson III
Edited by Timothy E. Parker

Copyright © 2010 Universal Uclick

ACROSS

1 Round number
5 Syringe contents, perhaps
10 ___ Helens, Wash.
14 Hosp. room
15 Metal in Montana's motto
16 Tibetan oxen
17 Ricky Ricardo was one
19 Berth place
20 Narrow inlet
21 They give a hoot
22 Lusters
24 Bring charges, perhaps
26 Shakespearean prince
27 Wastebasket, in jest
34 Spill the beans
37 Listing
38 Sauce type
39 Persia, today
40 Long journeys
41 Popular succulent
42 ___ Lingus
43 Big name in farm equipment

44 Lends a hood a hand
45 Legendary sleeper
48 Earnings on a bank acct.
49 Words sometimes said with a nod
53 Geological formations
56 Opera that opens in Memphis
58 It may provide a snug feeling
59 Wimbledon score
60 Type of clothing
63 One pushing a mouse around?
64 "Coffee ___?" (host's question)
65 Monkey wrench
66 Clothing category
67 Wrinkle with age
68 See-through item

DOWN
1 Striped quadruped
2 Web letters
3 Kidney-related
4 Former fort near Monterey
5 Erupting volcano, e.g.
6 Carrier to the Holy Land
7 X-ray units
8 Colorado native
9 Some law enforcement officers
10 Reflexive pronoun
11 Chaucer offering
12 Largest organ
13 Letters on measuring spoons

18 Enter one's password
23 Certain deer
25 The "dismal science," for short
28 Seven-time A.L. batting champ Rod
29 Where humans evolve?
30 Make a comparison
31 Seagirt land
32 Something to split
33 Some are behind glasses
34 One not to be believed
35 "... ___ saw Elba"
36 Ground cover
40 Circus or carnival attraction
41 Busy as ___
43 Hans Christian Andersen, by birth
44 Aquatic organisms
46 Some hollow-fanged snakes
47 "Bewitched" star
50 Steakhouse order
51 Davenport denizen
52 Zippy tastes
53 Live beneath one's station
54 Take it on the chin
55 Kind of thermometer
56 Animated film of 1998
57 Cannes brainstorm
61 Uris protagonist
62 Broadband choice

38 Double Dose

by Timothy Winton
Edited by Timothy E. Parker

ACROSS

1 Throaty utterance
5 Take, as a nonrequired course
10 Weather-beaten
14 Double-curved molding
15 Hawaiian veranda or island
16 Customary function
17 Consoling words
19 Sunset-tinged, perhaps
20 Dealer's employer
21 Partition
23 Hoisting device
26 Sailor's employer
27 Sap-sucking insect
30 Kanga's tyke
32 Aboveboard
35 Regulated item
36 Pester
38 Lennon's wife
39 Type of scene
40 Knocking noise
41 Legendary Mel of the Giants

42 Flood stage
43 No longer shrink-wrapped
44 Polish literature
45 Converges on
47 Cell letters
48 ___ Canyon National Park
49 Wickfield's clerk
51 Site for some rites
53 First satellite
56 Takes the floor
60 Duchess of ___ (Goya model)
61 Start of a joke
64 Far Eastern desert
65 Causing goose bumps
66 Flat-bottomed vessel
67 Nine inches
68 Published again
69 Pivot on point

DOWN
1 Campus military org.
2 Title with Khan (Var.)
3 Matches, as a poker bet
4 Dandy's topper
5 "Your Song" singer John
6 Di-dah lead-in
7 Vane direction
8 Pack member
9 Make a logical connection
10 Reach one's destination
11 Squeal of delight
12 Alternative word
13 Cervine creature
18 British author Blyton
22 Clothes holder
24 Evidence of a major impact
25 Palm Sunday salute
27 They intentionally make spots
28 Deep-space mission
29 "What a babe!"
31 Bone-related
33 Clownish act
34 Singer Lenya
36 Chance occurrence
37 Young fellow
40 1953 AL MVP Al
44 Things to run
46 Keep possession of
48 Initials may be carved in it
50 Tight-fisted one, in slang
52 Kind of resistance
53 Gives under load
54 Tumultuous sit-down
55 Word with skinned or bended
57 Word with kit or around
58 Raw silk color
59 ___ terrier
62 Canadian hockey legend
63 Kind of operation

1 Over Yonder

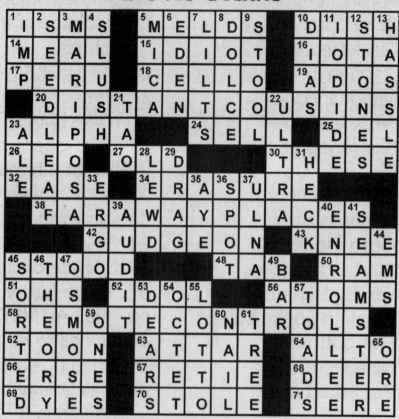

I	S	M	S		M	E	L	D	S		D	I	S	H
M	E	A	L		I	D	I	O	T		I	O	T	A
P	E	R	U		C	E	L	L	O		A	D	O	S
	D	I	S	T	A	N	T	C	O	U	S	I	N	S
A	L	P	H	A		S	E	L	L		D	E	L	
L	E	O		O	L	D			T	H	E	S	E	
E	A	S	E		E	R	A	S	U	R	E			
	F	A	R	A	W	A	Y	P	L	A	C	E	S	
	G	U	D	G	E	O	N		K	N	E	E		
S	T	O	O	D		T	A	B		R	A	M		
O	H	S		I	D	O	L		A	T	O	M	S	
R	E	M	O	T	E	C	O	N	T	R	O	L	S	
T	O	O	N		A	T	T	A	R		A	L	T	O
E	R	S	E		R	E	T	I	E		D	E	E	R
D	Y	E	S		S	T	O	L	E		S	E	R	E

2 It'll Grow On You

I	M	B	E	D		S	T	E	P		S	C	U	T
N	A	O	M	I		A	R	E	A		T	U	S	H
C	H	A	T	S		F	O	R	Y	E	A	R	S	I
A	R	S		C	H	E	T		P	R	Y	E	R	S
N	E	T	T	L	E	S		C	H	I				
		I	O	N		W	R	O	N	G	W	A	Y	
S	T	O	P	S		S	H	I	N		A	I	D	A
W	A	N	T	E	D	T	O	B	E	O	L	D	E	R
A	R	O	O		R	O	S	S		M	E	E	S	E
M	O	R	P	H	I	N	E		P	E	N			
		E	V	E		R	E	L	A	P	S	E		
M	A	I	G	R	E		L	O	R	E		L	A	N
A	N	D	N	O	W	I	A	M		T	O	A	N	D
C	O	L	A		A	D	Z	E		T	O	N	T	O
K	N	E	W		Y	O	Y	O		E	M	B	O	W

3 All in All

R	U	M	B	A		C	O	S	T	C	H	A	T
I	S	A	A	C		A	S	I	A	L	A	C	E
M	A	N	T	A		S	L	E	W	A	L	E	E
		L	O	C	K	H	O	R	N	S	W	I	T	H
R	E	I	N	I	N		R	Y	E	D	I	E
O	R	E		A	O	R	T	A		P	I	E	C	E
O	A	S	T		C	U	E		S	I	N
	S	T	O	C	K	E	X	C	H	A	N	G	E
	G	A	S		A	P	E		S	O	R	E
A	T	L	A	S		P	S	A	L	M		O	N	E
B	R	A		T	A	U		L	A	D	D	E	R
B	A	R	R	E	L	C	H	E	S	T	E	D
E	U	R	O		O	K	A	Y		T	R	E	T	S
S	M	U	T		H	E	R	E		E	M	A	I	L
S	A	P	S		A	R	M	S		R	A	L	L	Y

4 Place Your Bets

D	I	N	E		T	O	I	L	C	R	O	W	S
A	S	A	N		A	O	N	E	R	E	T	I	P
L	A	Y	S	I	T	O	N	T	H	E	L	I	N	E
I	N	S	U	L	T	S		H	A	S	A	C	O	W
		E	L	O		R	A	I	T	T
G	O	E	S	F	O	R	A	L	L		I	R	O	N
I	V	E		A	S	I	F		S	E	V	E	R	E
S	E	R	U	M		A	F	T		V	E	G	A	S
T	R	I	P	E	S		L	O	P	E		A	T	T
S	T	E	M		T	H	E	M	A	R	B	L	E	S
		A	H	E	A	D		P	E	A
O	N	A	R	O	L	L		P	A	S	T	D	U	E
R	I	S	K	S	E	V	E	R	Y	T	H	I	N	G
F	L	E	E	T		E	L	E	A		E	D	D	A
F	E	A	T	S		S	I	P	S		D	I	O	N

page 79

5 To a T

Across/grid answers:

PLIE · TOWS · START
RONA · ARAT · EAGER
OVER · LATE · EPOXY
PERFECTTENSE
SATUP · OSLO · ESP
LIAR · ENHANCE
CSA · SNIP · ALTAR
RIGHTTOBEARARMS
ANGEL · SLAM · ESE
GUINEAS · LAOS
SSE · DESI · NICKS
EXACTPAYMENT
UTTER · ROSY · PLEA
MOOLA · ERIE · ELLS
POESY · TESS · ROTH

6 Unpredictable

SLAV · ASHEN · MAZE
TAXI · STARE · ARIA
EVER · SAIGA · DENS
PASTPERFORMANCE
ULTRA · AMASS
ALLOYS · CONE
DOES · ECLAT · ELM
ISNOTAGUARANTEE
TED · ALARM · UNIT
BRED · PHRASE
CAIRO · SPLAT
OFFUTURERESULTS
MINI · SEPIA · ROOT
EROS · ANTES · EURO
RETE · FOSSE · STEW

Answers

7 Body Snatcher

```
P A S S █ S T A T S █ B E A S
A L E A █ T O L L S █ A X I L
J A W B R E A K E R █ S P R Y
A N N U A L L Y █ S T E E L █
M I I █ G E L D S █ E D D I E
A S N O T █ █ T H E █ I N A
█ W A R █ S E A █ S T E T
█ T O N G U E T W I S T E R
S O N S █ I V Y █ L E A
I O C █ O N E █ C R A B S
P L A T O █ R A R E R █ U R I
█ S M A S H █ M A N E A T E R
S H E S █ E Y E C A T C H E R
P E R T █ R E B E C █ M O D E
A D A Y █ S T A R T █ E R S E
```

8 Snake Sound

```
H A B L A █ T A P A █ T A C K
U N L I T █ B L O G █ O B O E
S T E V E N S P I E L B E R G
K I W I █ O P S █ Y E L P S
█ N A N █ F U R S █
S P A G H E T T I S A U C E
A I L █ O T H E R S █ R A R E
L O O P Y █ R A T █ F E R A L
T U N A █ M A S H I E █ P T A
█ S E R V I C E S T A T I O N
█ T A L E █ E R R █
T U T T I █ M U M █ I S L E
S P R I N K L E R S Y S T E M
A T O M █ I O T A █ A T E A M
R O D E █ D U E L █ P E P P Y
```

9 Great Ex-speck-tations

¹S	²P	³A	⁴S		⁵A	⁶C	⁷T	⁸O	⁹R		¹⁰P	¹¹A	¹²N	¹³T

Across answers:
- SPAS — ACTOR — PANT
- ARCH — CLARE — UTAH
- NORA — CALLA — TOPI
- PERIODCOS — TUMES
- INS — POOP
- CAT — ETCH — NEWEST
- ADAIR — AONE — INTO
- POINTOFNOR — ETURN
- ERGS — PEON — SHRUG
- SNAPAT — RODS — EMS
- EDIT — EEL
- DOTCOMBUSINES — S
- OBIT — IONIC — ATEE
- FORE — SNIDE — SLEW
- FEED — METER — HOPE

10 Brief Statements

Across answers:
- DISC — ATOZ — ASKS
- OREO — PROVE — SHOP
- TEAL — ACRES — CARE
- FLASHINTHEPAN
- TRAINEE — ONEND
- HERETODAYAND
- EMIRS — DANE — PBS
- SANS — TOMMY — CAIN
- ENG — LONI — TORSO
- GONETOMORROW
- ATLAS — NELSONS
- SHORTANDSWEET
- PEON — PERIL — LIME
- ERNE — SEEDS — ENOL
- NEST — EDGE — TGIF

11 Back It Up a Little

S	T	E	W			T	A	S	T	E				F	E	Z
U	R	S	A			A	L	P	H	A	S			I	R	A
M	O	T	H	E	R	E	A	R	T	H			R	A	P	
O	V	A			M	O	X	I	E			O	L	E		
S	E	T	U	P			I	N	A	R	R	E	A	R	S	
		R	E	M	I	S	S			T	E	N	D	R	I	L
			P	R	E			P	E	N			A	M	M	O
O	L	D			E	R	M	I	N	E	S		S	E	W	
D	U	R	A			E	O	N			G	U	T			
O	R	E	G	A	N	O			D	E	C	E	N	T		
R	E	A	R	R	A	N	G	E			K	N	O	W	S	
		R	A	M			B	O	M	B	E			V	I	A
R	B	I			O	V	E	R	E	A	R	N	E	S	T	
O	I	L			R	E	A	G	A	N			A	N	T	E
B	O	Y			E	M	E	N	D			B	A	S	S	

12 Letter-Perfect

P	R	O	L	E			D	O	C	K			I	B	I	S
R	A	W	E	R			E	L	L	A			N	O	R	A
A	N	E	A	R			L	E	A	N			A	L	A	N
M	I	N	D	O	N	E	S	P	S	A	N	D	Q	S		
			I	R	E			S	A	M	E					
R	A	I	N			E	R	A			S	A	L	A	D	S
A	W	N	S			D	O	N	E			S	Y	R	I	A
N	A	B			X	S	A	N	D	O	S			T	A	N
D	R	E	A	R			R	U	G	S			F	I	N	D
R	E	D	R	A	W			L	E	I			R	E	A	P
		B	Y	E	S			E	R	E						
D	O	T	I	S	A	N	D	C	R	O	S	S	T	S		
O	B	I	T			P	O	O	L			O	H	A	R	E
L	O	D	E			O	R	E	O			M	E	L	E	E
L	E	E	R			N	E	S	T			S	N	E	E	R

13 Ride Along

14 Have a Blast

15 Costs About a Grand

```
H A C K . R P M S . . I N A N E
A G U E . C A A N . R I G I D .
J U R Y C A N Y O N S T A N D .
I N T R O . A S W E . W R A Y .
. . . . I T E M . . S R I . . .
. C E N T R A L S T A T I O N .
H A N G A R . A P S E . N R A .
A R T S . . C P A . R E A R . .
I L E . L U A U . O V E R L Y .
L A R C E N Y P A R E N T S . .
. . L E I . . . N E R O . . . .
S P C A . T A M E . D U M A S .
P I A N O S L A M F I N A L E .
A L I G N . A S I A . C R O W .
T E N S E . S H A Q . E X E S .
```

16 Say-So

```
H U G E . I N S T E P . E L S .
O N U S . C A N I N E . R A E .
C O M P L E T I N G A . S U V .
. . D I E . O P T . H A R E . .
S U R E S T . . C R A T E R . .
C R O S S W O R D P U Z Z L E .
A S P . O P E R A T E . . . . .
M A S T S . E L I . S L A V S .
. . U P D R A F T . N E O . .
I S O N E W A Y T O G E T I N .
M E D I C I . . P L A I N S . .
P A D S . H A G . U R B . . . .
A M I . T H E L A S T W O R D .
L E T . B E R A T E . I D E E .
A N Y . A N D R E W . G Y M S .
```

17 Questions, Questions

T	H	I	S		C	H	A	S	E		B	L	O	B
D	U	N	E		O	I	L	E	R		A	O	N	E
S	L	A	P		C	L	E	A	R		C	M	O	N
	A	N	I	M	A	L	C	R	A	C	K	E	R	S
		A	R	C			S	T	U	B				
D	S	T		S	O	L	D		A	P	O	D	A	L
A	T	O	P		L	O	O	K		P	A	U	L	A
V	E	G	E	T	A	B	L	E	G	A	R	D	E	N
I	N	A	N	E		S	T	L	O		D	E	C	K
D	O	S	I	N	G		S	P	A	N		S	K	Y
			T	O	R	I		L	E	A				
M	I	N	E	R	A	L	D	E	P	O	S	I	T	
E	D	E	N		P	I	A	N	O		O	D	O	R
T	E	X	T		E	U	R	O	S		N	O	O	N
S	E	T	S		S	M	E	L	T		E	L	K	S

18 Deal Me In

C	H	A	R		S	H	A	R	P		R	A	M	P
H	A	L	E		C	A	N	O	E		E	R	I	E
I	V	A	N		A	N	T	O	N		T	A	C	O
C	O	T	T	O	N	G	I	N		U	R	B	A	N
O	C	E	A	N			E	S	S	E				
		L	O	N	E	L	Y	H	E	A	R	T	S	
D	A	B	S		O	V	A		O	R	D	E	A	L
U	F	O		A	V	A	T	A	R	S		S	K	I
A	R	R	I	V	E		E	R	E		S	T	E	P
L	O	N	D	O	N	B	R	I	D	G	E			
		C	I	A	O			P	A	S	S	E		
S	A	L	A	D		T	R	O	J	A	N	W	A	R
O	D	O	R		S	T	A	R	E		C	O	T	E
F	E	U	D		I	O	T	A	S		E	R	I	C
A	N	T	S		S	M	E	L	T		S	E	N	T

19 Start Me Up

F	L	A	R	E		I	S	A	S		H	E	M	P
L	I	N	E	R		P	U	L	P		E	V	I	L
O	A	T	E	R		S	M	E	E		A	E	R	O
P	R	I	V	A	T	E	O	X	A	N	D	R	E	D
		E	T	E		A	R	O	W					
P	A	M		A	T	O	P		S	L	I	P	U	P
E	R	I	E		O	V	E	R		A	N	O	S	E
C	O	M	M	O	N	I	C	E	A	N	D	O	U	T
O	S	I	E	R		D	A	D	S		S	L	A	T
S	E	C	R	E	T		N	O	P	E		S	L	Y
	G	O	R	E			E	L	I					
F	R	E	E	S	I	D	E	A	N	D	D	R	O	P
L	O	R	N		B	U	L	B		E	L	I	D	E
E	P	I	C		A	C	M	E		S	E	T	I	N
D	E	N	Y		L	E	S	T		T	R	E	N	D

20 Time Check

A	L	B	S		D	E	B	T		I	M	A	G	E
P	A	R	A		U	S	E	R		B	I	T	E	R
E	T	A	L		N	C	A	A		I	N	T	E	R
S	E	C	O	N	D	A	R	Y		D	U	N	K	S
	N	O	E	L		S	T	E	T					
B	A	N		T	E	A	L		O	M	E	L	E	T
O	M	A	H	A		T	A	S	S		M	I	L	E
R	I	C	O		S	O	D	A	S		A	R	I	A
E	C	R	U		T	R	E	F		G	N	A	T	S
S	I	E	R	R	A		N	E	M	O		S	E	E
	G	I	N	A		T	E	E	M					
S	C	O	L	D		D	A	Y	D	R	E	A	M	S
P	A	P	A	L		A	I	N	U		D	R	A	T
A	M	U	S	E		I	D	E	S		A	C	M	E
M	E	S	S	Y		R	A	T	A		L	O	A	M

21 Y Name Names?

```
B E S S · S A V E · S A J A K
E X I T · Q U I T · A D O R N
L A Z Y S U S A N · F O L I O
A M E L I A · N A M E · L E T
· · · E R R E D · E T H Y L S
G A B R I E L · F L Y E R · ·
I L L · U S A G E S · R O W S
R O O K S · T A D · R E G A L
L E O N · D E S O T O · E R A
· · D I M E S · R E D A R M Y
D A Y T O N · C A N E R · · ·
R U M · U T A H · S U G A R Y
E G A D S · S L O P P Y J O E
A E R I E · P O L O · L A V A
D R Y E R · S E A T · E X E S
```

22 Not Grade AA Meals

```
A G N E W · A E S O P · B R R
B R I N E · L A N K A · L E O
B A N A N A B R E A D · A V A
E D A M · D A L E Y · S C U D
· · O R E · · R E T A K E S
U M B R E L L A · D R I B ·
T A R · V E E R S · A N E A R
A D O R E · G E E · I T A L Y
H E W E R · S W E A T · N E E
· N E S S · E N D O R S E S
T A B L E T S · I R E · · ·
A L E S · E L A T E · G N A T
M I T · B E E F B U R R I T O
P E T · O P E R A · B E L O W
A N Y · A S T O R · I T E M S
```

23 Higher and Higher

A	C	H	E			D	A	C	E			R	U	R	A	L
C	L	A	M			O	L	A	V			O	N	O	N	E
R	A	I	S	E	O	B	J	E	C	T	I	O	N	S		
E	S	T			L	U	A	U			L	A	S	S	I	E
S	P	I	R	I	T		N	E	A	T	O					
			I	Z	O	D		D	R	O	N	I	N	G		
L	I	F	T	A	F	I	N	G	E	R		T	O	O		
E	R	I	E			L	I	E			E	T	O	N		
A	M	T		G	O	U	P	I	N	S	M	O	K	E		
D	A	S	B	O	O	T		N	O	T	I					
		E	T	H	E	L		E	A	T	I	N	G			
M	A	S	H	I	E		A	N	N	S		V	I	E		
A	S	C	E	N	D	T	H	E	T	H	R	O	N	E		
Y	E	A	S	T		S	T	I	R		O	R	E	S		
S	A	N	T	O		O	I	L	Y		E	Y	R	E		

24 Round We Go

D	U	M	B	O		A	R	U	B	A		D	I	S
I	S	A	A	C		R	E	A	L	M		A	N	T
M	O	T	H	E	R	E	A	R	T	H		I	D	E
			L	E	A	D		E	L	L	I	E		
S	A	W	L	O	G	S		S	A	R	O	Y	A	N
A	D	O	P	T	S		P	O	P	S	U	P		
B	E	R	G	S		E	R	U	P	T		L	S	D
L	A	L	A		O	P	A	R	T		F	A	I	R
E	L	D		S	L	I	T	S		C	O	N	E	Y
		S	E	L	E	C	T		S	L	E	E	V	E
S	T	E	R	E	O	S		T	O	A	S	T	E	R
C	O	R	G	I		I	R	O	N					
U	R	I		G	O	L	D	E	N	G	L	O	B	E
T	I	E		H	E	E	L	S		E	E	R	I	E
S	I	S		T	R	I	E	S		D	E	C	O	R

25 Cold Comfort

¹P	²O	³P	⁴S		⁵A	⁶D	⁷A	⁸M		⁹S	¹⁰T	¹¹E	¹²V	¹³E
¹⁴O	L	E	O		¹⁵R	I	T	E		¹⁶T	A	L	E	S
¹⁷M	I	E	N		¹⁸E	P	O	S		¹⁹A	S	S	E	T
²⁰P	O	L	A	²¹R	O	P	P	O	²²S	I	T	E	S	
			²³R	I	L	E		²⁴Z	A	N	Y			
²⁵D	²⁶U	²⁷E		²⁸V	A	R	²⁹I	O	U	S		³⁰A	³¹S	³²S
³³I	N	D	³⁴I	A		³⁵B	I	T		³⁶I	N	C	A	
³⁷C	H	I	L	L	³⁸Y	³⁹R	E	C	E	⁴⁰P	T	I	O	N
⁴¹T	I	C	K		⁴²A	H	A			⁴³I	S	S	U	E
⁴⁴A	P	T		⁴⁵G	R	E	M	⁴⁶L	⁴⁷I	N		⁴⁸E	R	R
			⁴⁹P	A	N	T		⁵⁰I	N	C	⁵¹H			
	⁵²C	⁵³O	O	L	S	O	⁵⁴N	E	S	H	E	⁵⁵E	⁵⁶L	⁵⁷S
⁵⁸F	A	T	A	L		⁵⁹R	O	L	E		⁶⁰I	C	O	N
⁶¹B	R	I	C	E		⁶²I	G	O	T		⁶³S	H	O	O
⁶⁴I	T	C	H	Y		⁶⁵C	O	W	S		⁶⁶T	O	M	B

26 Camera-Ready

¹R	²O	³S	⁴A		⁵S	⁶P	⁷R	⁸A	⁹T		¹⁰S	¹¹T	¹²O	¹³P
¹⁴O	P	E	C		¹⁵A	R	U	B	A		¹⁶P	H	I	L
¹⁷A	I	D	A		¹⁸F	I	D	E	L		¹⁹E	E	L	Y
²⁰S	N	A	P	²¹D	E	C	I	S	I	²²O	N	S		
²³T	E	N	U	I	T	Y			²⁴S	T	A	²⁵S	²⁶H	
			²⁷L	E	Y		²⁸T	²⁹R	³⁰A	M		³¹U	K	E
	³²M	³³A	C		³⁴C	H	I	L	I		³⁵R	I	M	
³⁶O	U	T	O	³⁷F	³⁸T	H	E	P	I	C	³⁹T	U	R	E
⁴⁰A	R	P		⁴¹A	W	A	R	E			⁴²E	S	T	
⁴³T	A	R		⁴⁴T	O	P	E		⁴⁵S	⁴⁶P	A			
⁴⁷S	L	E	⁴⁸W	S				⁴⁹S	P	I	R	⁵⁰E	⁵¹A	⁵²S
		⁵³S	H	O	⁵⁴T	⁵⁵I	⁵⁶N	T	H	E	D	A	R	K
⁵⁷O	⁵⁸R	E	O		⁵⁹A	D	O	R	E		⁶⁰U	R	S	A
⁶¹R	U	N	S		⁶²D	O	N	O	R		⁶³C	L	O	T
⁶⁴R	E	T	E		⁶⁵S	L	O	P	E		⁶⁶T	Y	N	E

27 It's Your Choice

¹A	²P	³S	⁴E		⁵S	⁶T	⁷A	⁸T		⁹O	¹⁰V	¹¹E	¹²R
¹³F	O	A	M		¹⁴T	Y	P	O		¹⁵C	I	N	E
¹⁶R	E	G	U	¹⁷L	A	R	O	R	¹⁸D	E	C	A	F
¹⁹F	I	T	S		²⁰E	T	A		²¹E	L	A	T	E
²²A	K	A		²³L	E	I		²⁴C	²⁵O	L	O	R	E	R
²⁶C	A	S	²⁷H	O	R	C	²⁸R	E	D	I	T		
²⁹A	N	T	E	S			³⁰A	D	O	S		³¹C	³²I	³³G
³⁴D	E	E	M		³⁵S	³⁶O	B	E	R		³⁷H	O	P	I
³⁸E	R	R		³⁹S	L	A	B		⁴⁰D	O	R	S	A
			⁴¹S	M	O	K	I	N	⁴²G	⁴³O	R	N	O	N
⁴⁴L	⁴⁵A	⁴⁶N	C	E	T	S		⁴⁷A	A	H		⁴⁸E	F	T
⁴⁹A	L	O	H	A			⁵⁰A	I	L		⁵¹E	R	A	S
⁵²P	A	P	E	R	⁵³O	⁵⁴R	P	L	A	⁵⁵S	T	I	C
⁵⁶I	M	A	M		⁵⁷W	H	E	E		⁵⁸R	A	N	T
⁵⁹S	O	R	E		⁶⁰L	O	R	D		⁶¹I	T	G	O

28 Box Office Poison

¹P	²P	³D		⁴E	⁵D	⁶D	⁷A		⁸S	⁹A	¹⁰L	¹¹A	¹²M	¹³I
¹⁴O	A	R		¹⁵D	R	E	W		¹⁶A	L	A	T	E	D
¹⁷S	H	E		¹⁸G	U	L	F		¹⁹N	E	W	E	L	S
²⁰S	L	I	²¹C	E	D	T	U	²²R	K	E	Y		
²³E	A	S	E		²⁴G	A	L	A			²⁵E	²⁶L	²⁷A	²⁸N
²⁹S	V	E	L	³⁰T	E		³¹R	³²A	³³T	R	A	C	E
³⁴S	I	R	E	E		³⁵O	³⁶N	E	O	R		³⁷B	E	T
			³⁸B	E	³⁹L	L	Y	F	L	⁴⁰O	P		
⁴¹A	⁴²S	⁴³H		⁴⁴T	O	I	T	Y		⁴⁵P	⁴⁶L	⁴⁷A	⁴⁸I	D
⁴⁹C	H	E	⁵⁰K	H	O	V		⁵¹M	O	U	S	S	E
⁵²T	U	N	A		⁵³E	⁵⁴R	⁵⁵I	E		⁵⁶M	F	O	R
		⁵⁷H	⁵⁸Y	⁵⁹D	R	O	G	E	⁶⁰N	B	O	M	B
⁶¹A	⁶²T	⁶³T	L	E	E		⁶⁴B	A	K	E		⁶⁵R	E	I
⁶⁶M	A	N	U	A	L		⁶⁷E	V	E	R		⁶⁸M	R	E
⁶⁹S	I	T	A	R	S		⁷⁰S	E	R	F		⁷¹E	S	S

29 Guys' Names

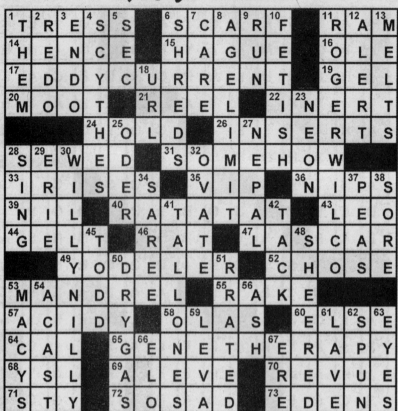

Crossword grid 29:

T	R	E	S	S		S	C	A	R	F		R	A	M
H	E	N	C	E		H	A	G	U	E		O	L	E
E	D	D	Y	C	U	R	R	E	N	T		G	E	L
M	O	O	T		R	E	E	L		I	N	E	R	T
		H	O	L	D		I	N	S	E	R	T	S	
S	E	W	E	D		S	O	M	E	H	O	W		
I	R	I	S	E	S		V	I	P		N	I	P	S
N	I	L		R	A	T	A	T	A	T		L	E	O
G	E	L	T		R	A	T		L	A	S	C	A	R
	Y	O	D	E	L	E	R		C	H	O	S	E	
M	A	N	D	R	E	L		R	A	K	E			
A	C	I	D	Y		O	L	A	S		E	L	S	E
C	A	L		G	E	N	E	T	H	E	R	A	P	Y
Y	S	L		A	L	E	V	E		R	E	V	U	E
S	T	Y		S	O	S	A	D		E	D	E	N	S

30 Author Unknown

Crossword grid 30:

B	A	N	D		C	L	O	D	S		S	T	I	R
O	D	O	R		R	I	V	A	L		P	U	C	E
N	A	V	Y		O	M	A	H	A		I	L	I	A
D	R	E	G		W	E	L	L	V	E	R	S	E	D
		L	O	O	N	Y		L	I	A	R	S		
O	N	I	O	N		S	O	W	H	A	T			
W	E	D	D	E	D		R	A	I	N		B	A	H
E	V	E	S		E	R	A	S	E		D	Y	N	E
S	E	A		W	A	I	T		S	T	I	T	C	H
			T	A	R	G	E	T		A	S	H	E	S
O	S	C	A	R			E	D	U	C	E			
C	H	I	L	D	S	P	L	A	Y		A	B	B	A
T	I	D	E		L	H	A	S	A		R	O	O	F
E	V	E	N		A	I	M	E	D		D	O	N	T
T	A	R	T		P	L	A	T	S		S	K	Y	S

31 Timespan

Across grid 31:
- S O N Y | A L O H A | S T A B
- O B O E | M O P U P | T U N A
- F I R S T O F T H E M O N T H
- A T M | H U T S | I N S E T
- P U N Y | M A L E
- A S S I S T | G O L D | B E E
- C L U E | P A U S E | R U N
- M I D D L E O F N O W H E R E
- E N S | A L O F T | A T O M
- S K Y | Y A L E | C U R T S Y
- A O N E | P A L E
- S K I F F | P I M A | G E M
- E N D O F T H E C E N T U R Y
- R O L O | H O N O R | W R I T
- A X E L | Y E N T A | O U C H

32 Let's Do Lunch

Across grid 32:
- A P E N | G A M A | A L A M O
- S E R E | O R E S | S A G A S
- H E R O W O R S H I P P E R S
- B W A N A S | H O R A S
- I E N | R E V | T A R | S E A
- N E T S | E A R | S A D I S M
- M A G P I E | G E N T S
- K I N G O F C L U B S
- H A I T I | R E L I S T
- A S T H M A | R A N | S E E S
- S S E | A N N | T E A | U R I
- S T E A L | S H I N E R
- Y E L L O W S U B M A R I N E
- O N A I R | A R I A | I C O N
- N E W T S | L E O N | S E W S

33 Go Forth and Multiply

N	A	R	C		G	R	A	M		A	L	I	V	E
O	L	E	O		E	A	S	E		R	I	S	E	R
T	E	N	C	O	M	M	A	N	D	M	E	N	T	S
A	C	T	O	R	S		P	S	E	C		T	O	T
		A	G	T	S		A	A	H	S				
B	S	C		S	A	C	S		L	A	L	A	L	A
A	L	A	E		T	A	P	S		I	O	N	I	A
H	U	N	D	R	E	D	Y	E	A	R	S	W	A	R
T	R	A	D	E		S	O	A	P		H	A	N	G
S	P	L	A	S	H		N	O	P	E		R	A	H
		S	H	A	M		F	L	A	B				
S	K	I		O	L	I	O		A	R	R	E	S	T
C	A	S	T	O	F	T	H	O	U	S	A	N	D	S
A	L	L	O	T		T	I	A	S		S	N	A	P
B	E	E	P	S		S	O	R	E		S	A	K	S

34 Rhyme Trips

A	M	F	M		A	T	T	Y	S		R	E	B	S
S	A	L	A		B	A	R	E	S		A	R	E	A
A	L	A	S		E	X	I	S	T		D	O	N	T
P	I	N	K	S	L	I	P	S		C	A	S	T	E
		U	S	E		I	M	P	R	E	S	S		
T	E	M	P	I		S	T	R	A	U	B			
U	B	O	A	T	S		H	E	M		L	A	B	S
B	O	O	P		H	O	R	E	B		I	D	E	E
A	N	T	E		I	V	E		A	P	P	E	A	R
	R	A	N	E	E	S		I	S	S	U	E		
C	A	T	C	H	E	R		A	A	A				
O	P	A	L	S		B	A	C	K	F	L	I	P	S
A	N	T	I		W	I	S	H	I		A	F	R	O
L	E	A	P		S	T	I	E	S		I	F	I	T
S	A	S	S		W	E	S	T	S		D	Y	E	S

35 Improving Steadily

S	H	O	D		A	S	C	O	T		B	E	L	G
H	E	R	E		C	H	O	S	E		A	V	E	R
A	R	E	A		R	A	I	L	S		B	E	T	A
G	O	O	D	F	O	R	N	O	T	H	I	N	G	S
			B	A	S	I	S			A	E	S	O	P
L	U	M	E	N	S			B	L	V	D			
A	R	I	A		A	L	T	A	R		E	R	A	
B	E	T	T	E	R	M	O	U	S	E	T	R	A	P
S	A	T		Y	E	A	T	S			A	N	T	E
		R	E	S	T			N	O	I	S	E	S	
O	S	T	E	O		S	E	O	U	L				
B	E	S	T	F	O	O	T	F	O	R	W	A	R	D
I	T	A	R		N	O	E	L	S		I	S	E	E
T	A	R	O		U	L	N	A	E		N	E	A	P
S	S	S	S		P	A	S	T	S		D	A	M	P

36 Mottled

L	A	M	A		S	L	I	N	G		D	A	D	S
O	V	E	R		A	I	D	E	R		A	B	E	E
D	O	T	T	E	D	L	I	N	E		S	H	E	W
E	W	E		S	L	Y		A	S	H	O	R	E	
		S	T	Y		G	U	T	T	E	R	E	D	
Y	E	N	T	A		G	U	N	N	E	D			
O	N	O	R		E	R	A	S	E		H	A	A	S
U	G	L	I		T	I	R	E	S		O	S	L	O
D	R	O	P		C	E	D	E	S		P	E	A	T
	E	L	E	V	E	N		G	E	A	R	S		
P	R	E	D	A	T	E	D		S	I	S			
L	I	A	B	L	E		D	O	M		E	T	E	
E	L	S	A		R	U	L	E	D	P	A	P	E	R
A	L	E	S		A	M	E	B	A		M	I	N	I
D	E	L	S		S	P	O	T	S		A	C	D	C

37 Cut and Dried

¹Z	²E	³R	⁴O		⁵S	⁶E	⁷R	⁸U	⁹M		¹⁰M	¹¹T	¹²S	¹³T
¹⁴E	M	E	R		¹⁵P	L	A	T	A		¹⁶Y	A	K	S
¹⁷B	A	N	D	¹⁸L	E	A	D	E	R		¹⁹S	L	I	P
²⁰R	I	A		²¹O	W	L	S		²²S	²³H	E	E	N	S
²⁴A	L	L	²⁵E	G	E			²⁶H	A	L				
			²⁷C	I	R	²⁸C	²⁹U	³⁰L	A	R	F	³¹I	³²L	³³E
³⁴L	³⁵E	³⁶T	O	N		³⁷A	T	I	L	T		³⁸S	O	Y
³⁹I	R	A	N		⁴⁰T	R	E	K	S		⁴¹A	L	O	E
⁴²A	E	R		⁴³D	E	E	R	E		⁴⁴A	B	E	T	S
⁴⁵R	I	P	⁴⁶V	A	N	W	I	N	⁴⁷K	L	E			
		⁴⁸I	N	T				⁴⁹I	G	E	⁵⁰T	⁵¹I	⁵²T
⁵³S	⁵⁴L	⁵⁵O	P	E	S		⁵⁶A	⁵⁷I	D	A		⁵⁸B	O	A
⁵⁹L	O	V	E		⁶⁰H	⁶¹A	N	D	M	E	⁶²D	O	W	N
⁶³U	S	E	R		⁶⁴O	R	T	E	A		⁶⁵S	N	A	G
⁶⁶M	E	N	S		⁶⁷W	I	Z	E	N		⁶⁸L	E	N	S

38 Double Dose

¹R	²A	³S	⁴P		⁵E	⁶L	⁷E	⁸C	⁹T		¹⁰A	¹¹G	¹²E	¹³D
¹⁴O	G	E	E		¹⁵L	A	N	A	I		¹⁶R	O	L	E
¹⁷T	H	E	R	¹⁸E	T	H	E	R	E		¹⁹R	O	S	E
²⁰C	A	S	I	N	O			²¹D	²²I	V	I	D	E	R
			²³W	I	N	²⁴C	²⁵H		²⁶N	A	V	Y		
²⁷A	²⁸P	²⁹H	I	D		³⁰R	O	³¹O		³²L	E	G	³³A	³⁴L
³⁵D	R	U	G		³⁶H	A	S	S	L	³⁷E		³⁸O	N	O
³⁹M	O	B		⁴⁰R	A	T	A	T	A	T		⁴¹O	T	T
⁴²E	B	B		⁴³O	P	E	N	E	D		⁴⁴E	D	I	T
⁴⁵N	E	A	⁴⁶R	S		⁴⁷R	N	A		⁴⁸B	R	Y	C	E
		⁴⁹H	E	E	⁵⁰P		⁵¹A	L	⁵²T	A	R			
⁵³S	⁵⁴P	U	T	N	I	⁵⁵K			⁵⁶O	R	A	⁵⁷T	⁵⁸E	⁵⁹S
⁶⁰A	L	B	A		⁶¹K	N	⁶²O	⁶³C	K	K	N	O	C	K
⁶⁴G	O	B	I		⁶⁵E	E	R	I	E		⁶⁶D	O	R	Y
⁶⁷S	P	A	N		⁶⁸R	E	R	A	N		⁶⁹S	L	U	E